WOOHOO!
WEALTH

For Ilana,

With Warmth a Woohoo!

Best wishes,

Cohi

WOOHOO! WEALTH

THE 7 PILLARS OF CREATING THE WEALTH YOU WANT AND A LIFE YOU LOVE

COLIN DRAKE, CFP®, RLP®

Carpe Vitam Press

Cover Design by Budi
Cover photo by Gary Yost
Interior design by Adina Cucicov, Flamingo Designs

Disclaimer: This publication is designed to provide accurate and authoritative information in regard to the subject matter covered. It is offered with the understanding that the publisher is not engaged in rendering legal, accounting, financial or other professional services. If legal, financial or other expert advice is required, the services of a professional person should be sought. This book recounts the author's views and experience and implies no guaranteed outcomes or success for the reader.

CFP®, CERTIFIED FINANCIAL PLANNER™, and federally registered CFP (with flame logo) are certification marks owned by Certified Financial Planner Board of Standards, Inc. These marks are awarded to individuals who successfully complete CFP Board's initial and ongoing certification requirements.

RLP® and REGISTERED LIFE PLANNER®, are professional designation marks owned by the Kinder Institute of Life Planning. This designation is awarded to individuals who successfully complete the Kinder Institute's initial and ongoing designation requirements.

ISBN-13: 978-0-9882285-1-1

To Maman for teaching me about Woohoo!
To Pops for teaching me about Wealth.

ACKNOWLEDGEMENTS

I offer my deepest thanks and appreciation to you, my sweet Rebecca, for your constant support and encouragement throughout this adventure. I love you.

Thank you, Delphine and Morgan, for your *joie de vivre*.

Thank you, Chloe, Joyce and Chad for the time and care you put into helping me with this book. I am so grateful for the thought and heart you brought to the task.

Thanks, Gary, for your ample photography talents.

Thanks, Budi, for the great work on the cover design.

Thank you, George Kinder, for generously allowing me the use of The Three Questions in this book.

And thank you to my tribe—you offer me the opportunity to give and be my best—to live from my Sweet Spot. You inspire me with your appetite for life and your dedication to creating success on your own terms.

TABLE OF CONTENTS

PROLOGUE

The Parable of the Mexican Fisherman

A small fishing boat docked in a tiny Mexican village. An American tourist complimented the Mexican fisherman on the quality of his fish and asked how long it took him to catch them.

"Not very long," answered the Mexican.

"But then, why didn't you stay out longer and catch more?" asked the American.

The Mexican explained that his small catch was sufficient to meet his needs and those of his family. It even allowed him enough to save money for his old age.

The American asked, "But what do you do with the rest of your time?"

"I sleep late, fish a little, play with my children, and take a siesta with my wife. In the evenings, I go into the village to see my friends, have a few drinks, play the guitar, and sing a few songs… I have a full life."

The American interrupted, "I have an MBA from Harvard, and I can help you! You should start by fishing longer every day. You can then sell the extra fish you catch. With the extra revenue, you can buy a bigger boat."

"And after that?" asked the Mexican.

"With the extra money the larger boat will bring, you can buy a second one and a third one and so on until you have an entire fleet of trawlers.

Instead of selling your fish to a middleman, you can then negotiate directly with the processing plants and maybe even open your own plant.

You can then leave this little village and move to Mexico City, Los Angeles, or even New York City! From there you can direct your huge new enterprise."

"How long would that take?" asked the Mexican.

"Twenty, perhaps twenty-five years," replied the American.

"And after that?" the Mexican asked.

"Afterward? That's when it gets really interesting," answered the American, laughing. "When your business gets really big, you can sell your company stock and make millions!"

"Millions? Really? And after that?"

"After that you'll be able to retire, live in a tiny village near the coast, sleep late, play with your children, catch a few fish, take a siesta with your wife and spend your evenings drinking, singing, playing guitar and enjoying your friends."

PREFACE

Why Am I Writing This Book?

I'm writing this book because I'm totally passionate about wealth and about living life.

I've spent the last fifteen years as a financial advisor to multi-millionaires. I'm a wealth manager and a Certified Financial Planner®. I've managed hundreds of millions of dollars for wealthy individuals, families, pension plans and estates. I've specialized in comprehensive financial planning—taking a look at a your entire financial picture to optimize it and align it with your goals.

I've been in "the trenches" with our nation's wealthiest, spending over 10,000 hours in meaningful conversation with them about their money, their lives, their hopes and their fears. I know about millionaires.

Moreover, I've made a passionate study of wealth for over twenty years. My drive to understand "What is wealth?" and "How do we become wealthy?" has taken me on a fantastic learning journey through numerous fields rife with answers: modern finance, behavioral finance, positive psychology, spirituality, appreciative inquiry, leadership, peak performance and neuroscience, to name a few.

I'm a life, wealth, and leadership coach through The Coaches Training Institute (CTI) and a Registered Life Planner® with The Kinder Institute. (Think financial planning meets life coaching.)

Finally, I have the good fortune of being wealthy and can share from firsthand experience.

What I've Learned

In my years helping the wealthy, I've come to see something that defies a major cultural belief that we have. From the time we are young, we have deeply ingrained in us this belief:

When we finally have the money, we'll be living the life we've always wanted to live.

Guess what? Horse phooey! Wrong. Negative.

> *"It is wrong to assume that men of immense wealth are always happy."*
>
> **John D. Rockefeller**

I can report from years of working with those who have crossed the proverbial "finish line" (having enough money) that this is a myth. Some wealthy people are living fantastic lives they love, and yet plenty are not.

In our culture we have a belief that *when* we have the money, _along with it_ will come the life we've always wanted.

Few have made the distinction between "it will come" and "I will have the financial _freedom_ to create it." There's a *big* difference.

If you believe "it will come", then you tend to wait for the money and be fairly passive in envisioning and creating the life you want. You will have this "just get me there" drive based on a faith that it will all be OK once you have the money.

If you recognize that "you'll have the *freedom* to <u>create</u> the life you want", then you've picked up on the important distinction: to *create*.

Living the life you want requires that you *create* the life you want. Money doesn't do it for you.

Money is wonderful. It's clearly hugely helpful. It offers massive opportunities. I wish lots of money upon everyone. And yet, let's be clear: money doesn't deliver.

Money brings the *potential* to *help* you have the life you want, but it does not *provide* it.

After years of practicing traditional financial planning, something felt off, for me. We planners have always felt we are doing great work if we successfully help grow our clients' net worth and hit their financial goals.

But after years of sitting with clients with fortunes who are stressed and worried, clients with total financial freedom who choose to do very little with it, clients who have more than enough wealth and only set out to earn more, clients who don't know their families but know their portfolios to the penny... the true question finally emerged for me:

So what!?

What's the point of helping people accumulate wealth if they don't translate that into a life they love?

All along, we've been aiming for the wrong target. Our whole financial industry is predicated on this: Help clients get the money, and they'll take care of the rest. They'll know what to do with it.

And I've seen, over and over again, that's just not the case. Sure, having more financial security, in and of itself, is preferable to having less. But is that it? What's the point?

The target is Woohoo! The target is loving life. Money is just one tool in our toolbox.

> *"Wealth is not his that has it, but his that enjoys it."*
> **Benjamin Franklin**

I've come to see this as a fundamental truth:

The only way to have the life you want is to know what that life is, and to plan for that life *at the same time* as you plan for having the money to fuel it.

My happiest clients have clear visions of what a fulfilling life looks like to them. For years they've been taking active measures to make that real and to live it. My most unfulfilled clients are those still focusing on higher portfolio returns with the hopes that an extra 1% return will also finally deliver well-being.

It doesn't work that way. In some ways you know that, but at the same time, it's really likely that you still hold the deep conviction that it'll all work out once more money is there. We're raised with that deeply ingrained cultural belief.

My Mission

I've spent the last seven years meditating in a remote cave in the Tibetan Himalayas, pondering the nature of wealth and its inexorable components. I've channeled a spirit entity named Manfoofoo, who has revealed to me the ancient truths of wealth creation. I've played endless rounds of golf with Warren Buffett, Bill Gates and Richard Branson (that guy can *golf!*), extracting from them the exact formula for success. And now I know. And I'm here to share it with you.

OK. You got me! I'm kidding.

Not surprisingly, how to create wealth is not a secret. It's not a closely guarded wisdom inaccessible to the masses. It's not one single truth available only to those who trek through the Amazonian jungle to an ancient temple, fighting off spiders, snakes and hostile guards.

Success leaves plenty of clues. The "how to" of wealth is widely available. All of the information and education you might need to transform your wealth and well-being have always been available and plentiful. We have Google and Amazon, for crying out loud!

You know that there is no one *right* answer. Like anything, it's a matter of engaging, with curiosity and intention, in the quest to better understand and cultivate these qualities that you want in your life.

I'm on a mission to teach what Woohoo! Wealth (which I'll soon define) is, and how you achieve it.

Why? Because it's staggering how few people manage to achieve both wealth and high levels of well-being. Why is that so damned elusive? Why is something that virtually everybody wants reserved for such a tiny percentage of the population? If you believe that the opportunity is available to just about anyone, what's everybody missing? Is it really as difficult as it would appear based on the success rate?

I know that it's hard and that people need help. I'm here to help. I'm on a mission to reclaim wealth. To break out of a system that is failing us miserably. To reform the way we teach and guide wealth creation. To help create financial freedom and vibrant life energy.

There Is a Better Way

You can't talk about money without considering life and you can't talk about life without considering money. Money touches just about every aspect of our lives. The two are so intertwined that it doesn't make sense to plan for one without planning for the other. Yet virtually the entire financial services industry has little or no interest, training or experience in bringing your life into the conversation. This book does that.

This book is about diving into the question, "If having enough money doesn't fulfill, what does?" without dropping the quest for money. Money is powerful fuel for fulfillment. It's full of potential, opportunity, and freedom. This book is not about denouncing wealth in any way.

It's about a *better way*. It's about the next evolution in wealth management, where we move beyond accumulating money for money's sake, and into planning for radiant aliveness, for life well-lived.

I've seen great financial plans lead to miserable lives, and I've seen great life plans without the financial juice to fuel them. I've also seen the extraordinary results of **holistic Financial Life Planning that integrates the vision of the life you most yearn to live with the financial plan to help make it a reality.**

I stand for your wealth and your aliveness.

I'm about "*joie de vivre*" and "*joie de* wealth."

My goal is to inspire you to find your Woohoo! Wealth, to instruct you in powerful and proven strategies, and to entertain you along the way.

My journey has led me to founding my own wealth management firm, Drake Wealth Management (**www.DrakeWealth.com**), which is dedicated to helping you thrive, financially and personally. I'm deeply and passionately committed to helping others find their own Woohoo! Wealth. It's my life's mission.

And it's led me to write this book for you, in which I share the core lessons I've learned on the quest for wealth and happiness. Herein, you'll find a fresh perspective and a wonderfully powerful approach to thriving, to having the money you want and the aliveness you are here to enjoy.

My Tribe

My tribe is full of people who have energy and want more; people with gifts and the desire to give them; people with passion and the hunger to direct it; and people with brains and the willingness to ask for help where they need it.

My tribe is full of people who want to live with purpose and mission. My people love money and want enough to supercharge their life and their mission. This tribe cares about health, love, aliveness, the earth, and each other.

This tribe loves to have FUN! This tribe is into the support of the community, and into stretching out of its comfort zone in the quest to grow. This tribe has a "game on" attitude. This tribe calls out, "Show me the MONEY! Show me the LIFE!" This tribe knows there is a better way and is all about learning it and applying it. This tribe has reclaimed our cultural definition of success to build our own compelling and energizing vision.

Does that sound like you?

Well then, come on in!

This Book

How do we create Woohoo! Wealth?

This book is going to answer exactly that for you. This is NOT a get-rich-quick book! But it IS a get wealthier quicker book.

It's about the art, science and psychology of creating Wealth and Woohoo! Money and happiness. Wealth and well-being. Thriving aliveness.

I'm going to offer you a really powerful framework you can use to create wealth. One that is designed to bring with it the Woohoo!, too.

We'll look at a step-by-step process of WHAT to do and HOW to do it. We'll also look at WHY you want to do it.

This book is going to focus on the fundamentals—call it Woohoo! Wealth 101. I could write a much longer book with more instruction about wealth planning, but my mission is to set us on the right path, starting with getting the fundamentals down. The goal is to build the most powerful foundation and framework we can.

If you are neither wealthy nor thriving, then this book will chart the course to both.

If you are wealthy, but not thriving, you'll find the missing ingredients here.

If you are thriving, but not wealthy, you'll find your wealth-building strategy within.

If you are both thriving and wealthy, read on to learn more about what you are doing right and how to take it to the next level.

This book was written for people who want to live passionately, for people who want enough money to fund a fantastic life, for people hungering to find and give the best of themselves, for dreamers who want a game plan, and for doers who want an inspiring vision.

We're going to look at why we are failing at wealth—why we are lacking in vitality.

And we are going to do something about it.

We're going to start this book (Chapters 1 through 4) by busting some of the most powerful myths about money and wealth. That's going to lay some groundwork so that we can then dive into clearly identifying *why* we want wealth (Chapters 5 through 7) and what it takes to create Woohoo! Wealth (Chapters 8 through 11). This latter part is a practical how-to guide. It's meant to deliver information (Oh!), to deliver revelation (Aha!) and to deliver suggested action (OK!).

Throughout, you'll find a powerful and proven strategy for creating the aliveness and wealth you desire.

Please know that this book is not for passive reading. It contains fun and powerful exercises designed to propel you down the road to Woohoo! Wealth. Do them. They'll make a big difference.

Ready? Let's go.

INTRODUCTION

Woohoo!

WoooooOOOOOooooohhhhhhooooooooOOOOO!!!!!!!!!! You know that feeling. I know you know it.

It's the sweet cry of aliveness—of delight, triumph and joy. It's a huge YES! called out to the world. It's the ultimate expression of gratitude for the gift of life.

It's life force running through your body that can't help but erupt into a declarative explosion of fulfillment in the moment.

It's the feeling you get when, at long last, you are locked in a kiss with your high school crush.

It's the feeling of launching off the end of the dock as you hurl yourself into a refreshing lake on a sunny summer day in your youth.

It's that feeling when you have just dropped down the face of a wave, tucked into the tube, surfed it fifty yards, then pulled out.

It's the deal you just closed where everybody involved wins.

It's watching your daughter deliver her school play lines with gusto, or hearing your son tell his friend, "my daddy is so fun."

It's being afraid to ask for something you really want—then asking—and getting it.

It's the spontaneous prank you play on your best friend that leaves you both in hysterics.

It's finally having the courage to ski that terrifying run and looking back up at it.

It's winning the game you put your heart into.

It's looking at your business' thriving bottom line.

It's the buzz you get from helping someone in just the way you were made to help.

It's finally writing your book.

It's not just peak experiences. Woohoo! isn't just about chest thumping, high-fiving energy. Woohoo! has a full range of expression. Woohoo! can be sweet and soft.

Woohoo! can be the deep resonance you enjoy from sitting quietly with your father. The sweetness that comes from simply being present, loving, connected, and appreciative.

It's also the joy of cuddling your daughter as she falls asleep.

Of showing a stranger kindness.

Of delighting your spouse with a gift you know he or she will love.

Of watching a sunset and not wanting to be anywhere else but right there.

Of letting yourself cry during a movie.

Of calling an old friend just to say you love him.

And indeed, Woohoo! can also be explosive—the deafening cry of "WOOOOOHHHOOOOOOO!!!!!!"

Ultimately, Woohoo! is waking up filled with the joy of life, having gratitude for your good fortune, being engaged in your life, and having positive energy radiating from you.

Woohoo! is ALIVENESS!

Woohoo! is THRIVING!

Woohoo! is PEACE!

Woohoo! is deeply knowing that you are living life—awake to the miracle of it, awake to the mystery of it, awake to the beauty of the grand experiment. Engaged! Reveling in the challenge of it.

Woohoo! is living the life you most deeply want to live.

Woohoo! is a state of being. It's a way you ARE as you pass through life. It's figuring out the rules of the game and mastering how you play. It's knowing that you are the creator of your life and owning that responsibility with relish.

Woohoo! is BEING the person you know yourself capable of being.

Woohoo! is you, turned up to 10.
Woohoo! is you, living at your most authentic and most powerful.

What are some of the signs of Woohoo?
ENERGY! Sparkly eyes; joyous voice; radiant health; smiles; peace; alertness; optimism; gratitude; generosity; creativity; patience; leadership; courage; vulnerability; authenticity; risk-taking; embracing challenge; and love.
Are you getting the picture here?
You love Woohoo!, right? You want that, right? That's how you want to live!
Woooohooooooo!!!

Wealth!

OK. So, that's the Woohoo! part of Woohoo! Wealth. Now onto the wealth part.

You want to be wealthy.

Whatever that word means to you—you want that. Picture, for a moment, all the wonderful images that you associate with the word "wealthy." Leave out any negative ones. Just see the good stuff. Got some of those in mind?

You want that! Go ahead—say it. "I want that."

If you are hedging, hemming and hawing, cut the BS—you want that. You'd be crazy not to want that for yourself, your family, and for everyone in the world. Like health, it is something you want.

Now, I'm not sure what specific images are coming up for you. Wealth is an abstract word. You may be having visions of Ferraris, caviar and mansions, or you may have pictures of free time to play with your child in nature.

Most people acknowledge that wealth has a component defined by money—and having plenty of it. And most people know that money alone is not wealth—you can be wealthy without having a lot of money.

You want enough money to feel free to live as you choose and to feel secure for the long run. Everybody wants that.

The Woohoo! Wealth Graph

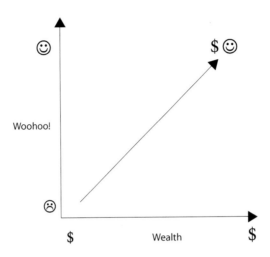

Take a look at the graph above. On the horizontal axis is money. Left means you have less money; right means you are richer.

On the vertical axis is Woohoo! Use any word you want for that: happiness, well-being, thriving, aliveness, or peace. The story is the same.

If we were to plot both your level of richness and your level of Woohoo!, we would put a point somewhere on this graph.

Where would you like it to be?

- A point in the **lower-left** means you have neither Woohoo! nor money. Bummer. (Sadly, most of the world lives here).
- A point in the **lower-right** means you are rich but aren't thriving (I think we all know people who are rich and miserable).
- A point in the **upper-left** means you are happy and poor (these folks might have a lot to teach us).
- Now, the **upper-right,** the promised land, the one way out in right field: Here, you have both money and Woohoo!, wealth and well-being.

ACTION

1. Draw a point representing where you feel you currently reside on the Woohoo! Wealth Graph (there's no scale on this one—just pick what feels right). Label that Point A.

2. Now draw a point where you want to be. Label that Point B.

3. Draw an arrow from Point A to Point B.

There! That's our game plan. Good job.

In the most simplistic terms, this book is about moving you up and right on this graph. From wherever you begin, it's really compelling to want to have more financial freedom and more radiant aliveness. This book is designed to help you achieve both.

CHAPTER 1

The Next Evolution in Wealth Management

Woohoo! Deficit Disorder

Holy smokes! Does the world have a case of WDD: Woohoo! Deficit Disorder! Look around! To quote the line from the movie *The Sixth Sense*…, "I see dead people!"

> *"Most people lead lives of quiet desperation and go to the grave with their song still in them."*
>
> **Henry David Thoreau**

I mean, really. Most people barely have a pulse! It's astonishing: they wake up tired; dread the day; go to a crappy job; complain about their boss; eat poorly; surf the "InnerWeb;" go home; numb out with food, alcohol, and TV; and stay up too late. Repeat. Blame circumstances out of their control.

That's not Woohoo! That's *Boohoo*!

Sure, we know some very vital people, some totally Boohoo people and all sorts in between. Yet it's amazing what the "average" level of aliveness around us is. It's alarming how few people we know who are truly *thriving!* Not just *happy*, but **thriving**.

How many people do you know who are "charged?" As if they have a fresh battery in them?

How many people do you know who are living life in their "Sweet Spot," using their greatest strengths towards their passions to make a difference they care about?

How many people do you know who have energy, endurance, joy and patience, engagement, creativity, and resilience?

How many people do you know who are really fun; who are an inspiration to friends, family, and colleagues; and who are living life to the fullest? How many people do you know who are playing the game beautifully, or whom you admire and whose Woohoo! you would gladly trade for your own?

Now think of how many people you know who are not like that.

Guesstimate the ratio of "Woohoos" to "Boohoos." Maybe 10% of people you know embody Woohoo?

Without a doubt, the overwhelming majority of people you know are not living in Woohoo! You may occasionally find them in that state, but wouldn't argue that they live there. It's more like their occasional vacation home.

So what! Not everybody can be charged! It's fine to be just OK! Right? That's one of the worst symptoms of WDD—no longer even having the *hunger* to be more alive. Being fine with fine. OK with OK. Comfortable with comfort. Really? With this one precious life, they're OK with mediocrity, living a life that was "all right"?

To be clear, Woohoo! certainly includes pain, struggle, challenge, defeat and suffering. It's not just about being happy all the time. It's more about total engagement in the full range of the human experience. And it's about conscious ownership of and gratitude for that experience.

It's about being alive. It's about widening the spectrum of your human experience to include higher highs, lower lows, and deeper fulfillment.

It's about amplifying your life energy—your aliveness.

ACTION

So, now that you have more of a definition of Woohoo!, here comes the big question:

Do you have Woohoo!? Is that you?

No qualifying. Check your gut. Are you the charged person I just described? On a scale of 1 to 10 (10 being supercharged), rate your Woohoo! in life.

Nobody's watching—just call it like it is. Don't attach any judgment to that—just notice.

When's the last time you actually wholeheartedly declared "Woohoo!" in your life?

And now… how do you feel about your level of Woohoo!?

Finally, pick a number from 1 to 10 where you would like to have your Woohoo!?

Please write your answers down.

Wealth Deficit Disorder

Here in America, in the land of the free, the home of opportunity, we have a massive case of another WDD: Wealth Deficit Disorder. Almost NOBODY in America becomes rich. Isn't that shocking? Let's look at some statistics:

- A 2011 CapGemini/RBC world wealth study reports that the U.S. has about 3.4 million millionaires out of a population of 311 million people. That means *only* 1% of the population accumulates $1 million or more (excluding home values). Sure, 3.4 million people is a lot of people on an absolute basis, but on a percentage basis, it's only about 1%.

- Only about 14% of Americans say they are very confident in their ability to retire comfortably. That's over 85% of Americas saying, "Not only am I not *rich*, I don't even think I can retire!"

- 60% of workers have less than $25,000 saved for retirement. How many years of retirement do you think that'll fund?

- Roughly 85–90% of people never become financially independent. They retire without enough money to support themselves and depend on Social Security and family.

- Roughly 93% of the nation's wealth (excluding homes) is held by the top 20%. In other words, 80% of the nation holds only 7% of the wealth. Ouch!

- A shocking 77% of workers live paycheck to paycheck, with no savings!

Can you believe that? Were you aware of that?

I could pepper you with pages of statistics, but let's keep it simple. We all dream of financial freedom, and very few of us ever achieve it, even here in the richest country on Earth.

ACTION

Take quick stock of your financial situation. Are you financially secure? Are you on track to financial freedom? How do you know? How do you feel about your answer?

Wealth AND Woohoo! Disorder?

So, if most people we know don't have much Woohoo!, and the odds of being wealthy are slim, what are the chances of having *both* Woohoo! AND wealth?

How many people do you know who are enjoying great financial security who are also really alive and thriving?

More importantly—are you?

The Financial Services Industry

It may or may not come as a surprise to you, but the wealth planning industry is not especially focused on helping you become wealthy. Here's why. For clients who have few assets, the industry is focused on selling products. These are usually commissioned mutual funds of dubious caliber. There's not much money to be made in helping folks who don't have much of it.

For clients with some assets, the industry provides some McDonald's-like portfolio management—usually cookie-cutter portfolios without a lot of personalized financial planning advice.

On the high end (portfolios of $1 million and up) the industry is less focused on creating wealth (the money's already there) and more focused on managing it. This may or may not include additional financial planning. There's plenty of profit and competition here. But really, the service is more about wealth "management" than wealth creation.

Generally speaking, the "worst" advisors tend to be the commissioned sales sharks from the big brokerage houses, and the "best" tend to be independent Registered Investment Advisors (RIAs) who are also Certified Financial Planners® (CFPs) working on a "fee-only" (non-commission) basis (getting paid for their time and/or assets under management).

But even if you get a "good guy," chances are that their training is going to be almost exclusively in helping you with the tactical strategies of saving and growing your portfolio. That's great, but wealth creation is about 80% "inner" game (mindset and psychology), and 20% "outer" (strategic) game.

> *"Wealth—any income that is at least one hundred dollars more a year than the income of one's wife's sister's husband."*
>
> **H. L. Mencken**

Who's teaching us HOW to become truly wealthy?

Most advisors just aren't trained in having the conversation with you about what true wealth looks like for you, and in helping you get there. The best that most offer is asking what goals you might already have and then crunching numbers to help you achieve those goals. But those goals tend to be generic ones such as paying for college tuition, paying off the mortgage, or retiring at age 65. My years of work with the wealthy have taught me that accomplishing those is wonderful, but isn't what life's about.

Ironically, the financial industry is advertising all about "dreams" and "focusing on what's important," yet delivering very poorly or not at all on that promise. I mean, really—when a big bank is selling you *checking accounts* with slogans and imagery about living the dream, don't you scratch your head and wonder, "Wait a second, how is my checking account going to help me live the life I want?" And does the bank teller sit you down and ask you about your vision of a fulfilling life? C'mon.

Advertising agencies know that you are hungry to live your dreams, but they aren't making sure the financial services industry is helping you realize them.

As a nation, we are being sold that the solution to our problems lies in higher investment returns from stock picking and market timing. That's bunk—returns are not at all the problem, and just about all evidence points to the fruitlessness of stock picking and market timing, anyway. But that's the main "product" being sold by the financial industry. "Work with us, and we'll know which stocks to pick and when to pick 'em. And then you'll be rich and happy." Even the more appropriate solution, an intelligently designed portfolio, doesn't solve our problems. It's a helpful tool in growing our net worth to fuel our financial goals. But that's it.

Can you feel it?

Forces are shifting. People are tiring of the empty promise of consumerism. People are devastatingly disappointed with our financial system and its leaders. We are being let down by our wealth advisors. We're tired of not knowing whom or what we can trust. **We're being let down by the conventional wisdom and the traditional path to "wealth."**

I see so many people weary of the "rat race," of being clobbered by being overscheduled, of grinding to keep up with the Joneses, and looking tired and empty. Life seems to keep getting busier, but we don't necessarily feel any closer to having the life we want. We're tired of being tired. Like kids calling from the back seat on a long road trip, our spirit calls out, "When are we going to get there?"

At the same time, plenty of people are doing just fine. They're enjoying success and the comforts they've expected to enjoy in life. It's all pretty darn good. By most measures, it all should seem fine. Yet there's still something missing. Even with the good job, the nice house, the sporty car, and the kids in a great school, it all adds up to something missing. A restless stirring in the soul asking, "Is that it?"

> *"For it is often the human condition to comply obediently at first, then to assert but still cooperate and compromise, then, finally, to discover choice, calling, maturity, and heightened drives for freedom, expression, and contribution. The Charged Life, then, usually calls to us after we have done what we were supposed to do, become who we thought we were supposed to be, lived as we thought we were supposed to live. Then the safety and comfort and compromise get to us, and a stirring of restlessness and revolution sends us off in search of greater adventures and meaning."*
>
> **Brendon Burchard**

There is a new consciousness emerging, and people are yearning for deeper wealth, for more full aliveness, and for living with higher energy. People crave to make a living doing what they love. To do well by doing good. To *give* their best while *being* their best.

We all want to believe that as we skid into our coffin, we'll be thrilled with and proud of the life we lived.

The rules and values our parents' generation lived by don't work for us—we're not living in the same world they were in.

We want it all—we want the money to live, and we *really* want to LIVE! We want to bring money to our lives, and life to our money.

The next evolution in wealth management is all about thriving finances and a fulfilling life.

CHAPTER 2

Money and Happiness

It's Not the Money We Want

Please consider this simple choice—which would you rather have?

A. $25 million. And on this $25 million (and all of your money) is a curse that guarantees that no matter how you spend your money (for yourself or others) it will never bring you (or others) any pleasure. It is rendered totally neutral—powerless to bring you any fulfillment, happiness, joy, meaning, or health. You can buy a mansion with it, and it will make you no happier than a shack would; you can travel to Europe, and it will bring you no joy. A fancy meal tastes the same as a microwave dinner. And let's even add that the money actually brings you an increasing sense of malaise for every dollar you spend.

Or…

B. You'll have just enough money to provide for your survival needs and robust health. You will live a life of deep fulfillment, of radiant energy, of passionate purpose, and of generous giving of your time, energy, and love. You'll use your particular strengths and gifts to impact the world, and you will know the joys of having loving friends, family, and community. Your life will include challenges that help you grow. You will forever be filled with a deep gratitude for the gift of life.

OK. Pick one. Again, no qualifications, just pick one.
Most people are going to go for B.
Simplistic? Sure. Nonetheless—here's the lesson…
Without the power to further our journey towards pleasure, meaning and fulfillment, money is useless. We only want money as a *means to that end*. We want if for what we <u>believe</u> it will make possible for us. Choosing option B above should illustrate this for you.

It's not the money you want, it's what you *believe* it will bring you that you want.

Yet in our culture we are much more conditioned to seek the money than that which it will ultimately afford us. We take as truth and on faith that the money *will* deliver that which we ultimately want from it.

Ok. So, hold that as a truth, for now: "it's not the money I want, it's what I hope the money will bring me that I want."

And That Would Bring Me…

When you get right down to it, here's the model we are taught in our culture:
Get money so that you can buy things and experiences, so that you can be happy.

You want a way to experience that? Try this:

ACTION

Please reflect on this statement:

If I had WAY more money than I do now, I would…

Now write down the first 5–7 answers that come to you down the left side of a sheet of paper.

> For example, "I would… buy new clothes, pay off my credit card, travel to Costa Rica, get a new car, pay for the kids' private school, etc."

Please do that before reading on.

Good. Now, to the right of each response, complete this sentence:

> **"… and *that* would bring me… "**

> To continue our example: "If I had WAY more money than I do now, I would… buy new clothes… and that would bring me… *a sense of looking good and feeling attractive… "*

Got it? Please do that for each of your answers before continuing.

When you are done, **do it again**, answering, **"… and *that* would bring me… "** for what your **second** column of responses would bring you.

To continue the same example: "If I had WAY more money than I do now, I would… buy new clothes… and that would bring me… a sense of looking good and feeling attractive… and that would bring me… *a sense of confidence… "*

In other words, answer what you would do with more money… and what that would bring you… and what *that* would bring you, etc., until you can't think of anything more it would bring you. That is, go until you've reached the end of the line—the highest concept (or perhaps an endless loop like, "and that would bring me joy, which would bring me peace, which would bring me joy).

Get it? Good. Please go ahead.

People's answers to this exercise tend to converge on a few key words—a few core things that they believe having more money will bring them. Perhaps the most common are "… and that would bring me happiness" (or happiness, or fulfillment, or peace, or love), or "I'd be truly alive" (or secure, safe, included, belonging, or loved).

What were your core answers?

In doing this extrapolation exercise, we've just uncovered what it is that you ultimately *believe* money will make possible or real in your life. By simply asking the equivalent of "what do you want from your money?" and repeatedly following up with "and what will that get you?" you likely unearthed some core money beliefs.

Most people seldom look past wanting the car, the clothes, the education, or the trip, to ponder: "and what will *that* bring me?" They tend to stop at just "wanting that."

And you know what? **We're all spending money with the unconscious belief that it will make us happy or secure.** We hope that through this chain of what money will bring us, it will ultimately bring us happiness.

But if I ask you: does money make people happy? you'll either answer, "no," or "it helps." And here is the key to this whole thing: We hold the conscious belief that "Money doesn't buy happiness," while we unconsciously and concurrently believe that anything we use money for *will* ultimately deliver us to a state of more happiness. We hold these contradictory truths—we *know* money won't make us happy, yet we *act* as if it will. And because deep down we *believe* it will, we want money—more of it—because we're pretty darn sure that with more of it we'd be happier. Deep down, it seems we believe that money doesn't buy *other* people happiness, but it probably would buy *us* happiness.

Is that making sense to you? It's an important concept to get.

And here's why:

We don't want to be rich. We want to be happy.

Want to check? Make the choice again: I'll grant you the wish to be either rich or happy, but you only get one. Which do you take? Happy, right?

The problem: **deep down, we believe that being rich will make us happy. So, rather than working on getting happy, we work on getting rich.**

Now, there's a good chance that right now, your brain is saying: well, yeah! Just get me rich and don't worry, I'll be happy! I'll know *exactly* what to do with it. I'll be fine. Forget the Woohoo woowoo mumbo jumbo; just show me the *money!!!*

What makes you so sure? Really. Don't you think that all of the multi-millionaires I've worked with would have thought that too? Aren't you wealthier now than you used to be? How well has that increased wealth translated into the fulfillment you're seeking in life?

Again, 99% of people won't get rich. And of the 1% that do, a minority will really be thriving. The odds are against you winning with this strategy of "just get me the money, and I'll be happy." If this were a game in Vegas, people would laugh at you for even approaching that table.

> **In working with and studying the rich for years, I've seen clearly that more money does not equal more happy. It doesn't necessarily mean *less* happy; it just means that there is *little correlation*.**

More and more research is confirming that after a certain threshold of household income, additional income doesn't contribute to additional happiness. Figures vary, but a recent Princeton University study illustrated that while increasing U.S. household income did translate into better daily moods, that effect tapered off entirely above the $75,000 a year mark.

You might be saying, "well, money doesn't make you happy, but it sure helps!" Absolutely. I'm not arguing that money doesn't play a big role in fueling our happiness. Again, I wish for you lots of money to help you live beautifully. And that's why a large part of this book is about how to build wealth.

The point I'm making is that most of us are acting on unconscious faith that when the money shows up, when we've finally banked it, the happiness part will be taken care of—it doesn't work that way. We're over-relying on the *means* rather than really asking, "How do I get the *end*? What *IS* the *end*?" Is there a shorter route; a more *certain* route? Where can money help, and where is it powerless?"

The reality is this: what we are seeking in life is to **_feel._** Virtually everything we do is in the quest for a feeling. We want money so that we can *feel* aliveness; *feel* happy. We want money so that we can *feel* free to have lives we love.

We want money so that we can feel Woohoo!

"I'll feel alive once I have enough money." That's always been the plan once we finally have enough. "Then I'll really start living. I'll live how I want. I'll be free, and then I'll have the means to make choices that really bring me alive. I'll really live life then!" That's pretty much our national game plan. But it's a terrible plan.

"Wealth is the ability to fully experience life."

Henry David Thoreau

Sure, we have Abraham Maslow's hierarchy of needs, and we certainly need money for food, clothing, shelter, etc. On that, most of us can agree (though there is a growing movement of people who willingly give up using money in their lives and are getting by just beautifully).

What I'm talking about in this book is our desire to go beyond our basic needs and become rich. Our desire to be rich is our desire to be free. Our desire to be free is our desire to be alive. So when you get right down to it, wealth planning is freedom planning. Wealth planning is aliveness planning.

Wealth planning is about designing fulfillment and then solving the financial pieces needed to fuel that fulfillment.

Most people take the approach that wealth planning is planning to have lots of money, and yet they don't really get into HOW that will translate into what it is they REALLY want? You see the problem?

Are you, by any chance, thinking, right now, "Well this doesn't describe me—don't believe I want money to be happy and alive"? If so, that's great. Still, I ask you this:

Are you as alive as you ever plan to be in your life?

If so, and assuming that you are a radiant being, Bravo! If not, when is it that you plan on becoming that person? Is there any chance that it's once you have the time and money?

The thing that we want money for is to be free, alive, and fulfilled. So, let's focus on that!

Let's paint the picture of what fulfillment looks like for you, figure out how much that's going to cost and then how to create that money.

Doesn't that make a lot of sense? Isn't that logical?

When you have the money *and* the fulfillment, you've got Woohoo! Wealth.

> *"My poor dad often said, "I'd rather be happy than rich." My rich dad said, "Why not be both?"*
>
> **Robert Kiyosaki (author of Rich Dad, Poor Dad)**

Wealth planning is fulfillment planning. Fulfillment starts with knowing what you really want. So, let's make sure to figure out what you really want!

But let's also be realistic: this is a lifelong pursuit. You may not find your whole answer here, and that's fine. Getting a compass heading is a powerful start.

Further, we'll probably never *fully* figure out what we want and truly get there. We'll never be "done," complete, or totally fulfilled. What we want, who we are becoming, will evolve over our entire lives. As soon as we get close to our vision, it will transform into its next higher evolution.

That's a great thing! Having a vision of aliveness and wealth guides us, grows us, and fulfills us. That vision is of what we most deeply want in this one life, what our soul craves to experience, create, and express. Because we can grow forever, there will always be a target ahead for us, and that vision is one of the greatest gifts of existence. It's a "guiding light."

Money Versus Wealth

As we dive into the discussion about building wealth, let's make a really important distinction. What's the difference between money and financial wealth?

Try this question on for size: before money was invented, could you be wealthy? Of course you could! Your wealth could be measured in resources—food, cattle, land, children, warm clothing, shelter, strength, the ability to create, etc.

Or, if you are alone in the middle of a desert holding a bag with a million dollars in it, are you wealthy? Nope—the money is useless. And you have no other resources to get you what you want and need (food, water, sun protection and a way out of the desert).

If you had no money but had a magic lamp that would grant your every wish, would you be wealthy? Absolutely—you could get anything you wanted and needed.

You might simply think of wealth as potential.

Wealth is the potential, stored up in some form, to have what you want or need.

If you want a trip to Tahiti, do you need money? Nope—you just need to have the potential to have that. If Uncle Ned calls to say, "I need to get rid of this darn trip to Tahiti I don't want—do you want it?" you have wealth. You have the potential to get what you want.

Wealth might be in the form of an asset that can be traded for what you need (e.g., "Here, take my watch in exchange for your shoes" or "Take this chicken in exchange for some corn"). It might be in the form of an entitlement (e.g., "You are welcome to use our ski cabin *anytime*— please do").

Of course, it can also be in the form of money.

Money is a way to move wealth around.

Wealth so often gets *translated* into money that we've learned to put all our focus on the *means* and believe that it holds the inherent value. Wealth actually has little to do with money. Money is a human invention, and a recent one at that. Its function is simply to facilitate the exchange of value. Rather than trade chickens for corn, we can trade chickens for a "marker of value" upon which everyone agrees.

We used to use rare and portable metals for this function—they were perfect for carrying around. It was hard to find your own metal. Eventually, we created more convenient paper currency and coin denominations to facilitate the exchange of goods and services.

Money facilitated *specialization* such that one person could focus on medicine, and another on baking. If the blacksmith needed bread, but the baker didn't need a sword, it could all be worked out through money.

Our currency used to be backed by something of inherent value when we were on the gold standard. You could indeed exchange your paper bills for a bag of gold, which everyone agreed was valuable and would be willing to trade for. Now, of course, we have gone off of the gold standard and have what is called a *fiat* currency—fiat, as in *faith*. It's backed only by the promise of the government to make good on it. There are lots of books and websites warning of the dangers of a fiat currency—there has never been one fiat currency in the history of humankind that has survived. Many argue that our U.S. currency is doomed to fail as well. Google "fiat currency" if you want to learn more. It's important to open your eyes to this potential reality.

Money is simply an agreed upon, but inherently valueless, method for exchanging wealth. Most *wealth* gets converted to *money* before being re-converted into another form of *wealth*. Crops get turned into money, which gets turned back into seeds or tractors. Wealth—money—wealth.

Money holds the potential to get us what we want and need because everybody agrees to use that as the common language of exchange. The only wealth in money is our common agreement to use it and the faith we have in the government. Beyond those two tenuous conditions, money is paper and metal, and its only inherent value is the utility value of paper (fire starter, anyone?) and metal (paperweight, anyone?)

Stock isn't money; it's the value of a business. Bonds aren't money; they're the value of the promise to repay you. Real estate isn't money; it's the value of the land, building and income it generates.

We are not out to build your money; we are out to build your wealth. And you'll do plenty of translating of your wealth into and out of money. They've effectively become interchangeable, but we must not lose the distinction.

It's not the money you want, it's the wealth.

Further, it's not the wealth you want; it's the potential to get what you want and need that you seek. It's the feeling of aliveness and security it can bring you that you want. And there are other really powerful routes to security and aliveness that don't rely upon money as the means.

CHAPTER 3

Life

"Is the life I am living the same as the life that wants to live in me?"

Parker J. Palmer

Life is a process of starting whole and pure; then getting beaten up and dented, and losing our way; then healing and finding our way home. We start innocent, perfect, and heavenly. Then life happens to us. We get shaped by experiences, family, society, culture, and the times; and we increasingly lose touch with who we are, what we want, and lose our inspiration to dream.

Then, at some point (if we are lucky), we begin to wake up, lick our wounds, reclaim ourselves and our lives, and declare to the world with purpose, passion and energy who we authentically are and what we are here to do.

Each of us has a radiantly alive and loving self yearning to be expressed. Each of us has a unique makeup that craves to express itself in the world in its authentic way. You are different from every person who has ever lived in the history of mankind and who will ever live again. And along with that uniqueness come a special concoction of experiences, interests, strengths, perspectives, virtues and desires that only you have, and gifts you are here to deliver to the world.

> *"The meaning of life is to find your gift and the purpose of life is to give it away."*
>
> **Joy J. Golliver**

Most of us just aren't that clear on our unique set of strengths and passions, and the difference we want to make in the world. That's in part because we are more conditioned to conform and lay low, to keep our head down and keep working, than we are to burn bright and "let our freak flag fly."

And, in that, we have our *fundamental* calling in life: to find what I call our "Sweet Spot." When we've found our Sweet Spot, we've found that place where we are using our greatest strengths (our unique gifts) and applying them to something about which we are passionate (we love it—it engages, fascinates and energizes us), and we are making a difference (an impact, that we find meaningful). And we are authentically ourselves. We're "home."

Wealth planning is Sweet Spot planning: find it, own it, live in it and give from it. We'll explore that further in Chapter 9.

Feeling the Hunger, Feeding the Hunger

You get hungry. What is hunger? It's an internal system you have that *knows* it needs something for survival. It sends you **signals** as *notification* to eat and creates **discomfort** as *incentive* to eat in order to heighten your chance of survival.

Well, guess what? You have another internal system doing the same thing. Call it spirit, soul, heart, divinity, higher self, inner knower, or whatever you want. There is some essence in you that has yearning, that has desire. It has forever sent you **signals** and notification (in the form of yearning, dreams and wants) and **discomfort** (in the feeling of pain, emptiness, meaninglessness, purposelessness) in the hopes that you would heed the call. That's because there is something in you yearning to live, to be expressed.

The renowned author Wayne Dyer puts it this way: you are not a human being here to have a spiritual experience. You are a spiritual being here to know itself through the human experience. Your desires are actually the desires of the spirit, the divine self. Your desires are SACRED!

Maslow put it similarly, stating that our ultimate quest is that of self-actualization, of transcending, of becoming who we are capable of being.

One of my teachers, Chuck Roppel, put it this way: Who are we? We are *consciousness* revealing itself in the human form with the *capacity to choose*. Our life purpose is to awaken the authentic self by choosing. And, as professed in just about every spiritual tradition, our essential nature—our authentic self—is peace, love, joy and compassion.

The point here is that when you listen, and allow yourself permission, you will hear something deep within you, calling. And this yearning is a good and beautiful thing. It's your guiding light. It's your calling. Those who have answered their calling have forged the history of the world.

Sadly, our time is one in which we aren't especially attuned to this inner voice, or to feeling the wisdom in our wanting. We too often lack the ability to sense this *creative* impulse. So, many have lost the capacity to dream or the energy to wish.

That is, in large part, because it's an enormously vulnerable thing to do—once you declare what you really want, you leave yourself open to the pain of not getting it, the ridicule of being judged, and the humiliation of failure. On top of that, we don't really have leaders or mentors who cultivate that capacity in us.

Additionally, we are massively programmed to want what others want us to want. TV commercials don't interrupt programming to encourage you to consider how your particular talents and passions can create value for others. As if! They plant, with masterful technique, the desire for what they are selling, over and over again—a tidal wave of telling you what to want and how you will benefit from it. So much so that lots of people give up looking inside for what they want and just give in to being conditioned by media, business, and society.

> *"Too many people spend money they haven't earned, to buy things they don't want, to impress people they don't like."*
> **Will Rogers**

I love this analogy from my colleague Rick Tamlyn, author of a great book, *The Bigger Game*: When we get physically hungry, a lot of us just grab the easiest thing, the tastiest thing, the nearest thing, the usual thing or the cheapest thing, typically empty calories, to make the feeling of hunger go away. We try to rid ourselves of that discomfort. And too few of us are driven by the question, "what is the nutrition that my body is craving and that will foster thriving health?"

Similarly, when our "spirit" sends us its hunger pangs, we make that discomfort go away with "empty calories" for our spirit: We watch TV; we numb the feeling with food, alcohol, drugs, sex, or shopping; or we distract ourselves with busyness. And we become accustomed to doing that. It becomes normal. Too few of us ask, "what is the "nutrition" that my spirit is craving and that will foster its thriving?"

Hearing your calling, listening to your yearning, is a skill that needs to be redeveloped (yes, *re*-developed, because as a kid you were a *master* at it).

Your life depends upon it! Your ability to hear what your deepest wants are will absolutely determine the quality of your life and how wealthy you ever become.

ACTION

Take a moment to ask: "What nourishes me deeply?" Which:
- Foods
- Activities
- People/Relationships
- Work
- Places
- Mindsets

Now, ask yourself: "What's calling to me?" What are you hungering for? What is it that you feel a consistent yearning for? What nourishment has been calling to you for a long time? What's happened when you've answered? What's happened when you haven't?

Spirit Vs. Ego

If you pay attention, you'll likely notice that you have two places inside you from which you desire. We'll call one your "ego" and the other, your "spirit." Your ability to distinguish the voice of your spirit from the voice of your ego will have an enormous impact on your life. Your ego has massive yearnings, constantly being expressed. They come from a different place within you and serve a very different purpose from the cravings of your spirit.

Your ego is a force in you whose main job it is to keep you safe. It wants security, approval, belonging, status, and status quo. It wants your survival, and is happiest when you are well fed, well protected, and flying under the radar. It doesn't want you to stick your head up or your neck out, it doesn't want to feel vulnerable, and it doesn't want you to risk being banished from the tribe. It wants to be *in* the tribe, and to have high social ranking within it. Because this is where it's safest. It does not want to leave its comfort zone.

Interestingly, there are strong evolutionary justifications and neurobiological bases for this. For a great part of evolution, humanity has been tribal, and the individual's survival has quite literally depended on remaining in the tribe. Survival for lone wanderers was much less likely than for those in the comfortable fold of the tribe. Behavior likely to lead to expulsion from the tribe has not been rewarded evolutionarily. Society has changed since those times, but our evolutionary programming and wiring hasn't kept up.

We are still scared shitless of being rejected from the tribe (society). It's probably our greatest fear. Fascinating studies illustrating this have been done where several people play a computer game in which they virtually throw a ball amongst themselves onscreen. There is one subject (i.e., "sucker"), and the rest of the players are in on the experiment. Soon after starting, they stop "throwing the ball" to the subject. Even in this meaningless virtual game, this act of "expelling the subject from the tribe" induces very real and measurable indicators of stress in the subject (such as sharply increased Cortisol levels). We're *wired* to fear rejection.

And thus, this force within us, the ego, wants to belong and wants to fortify its safety. How does this express itself in the real world? Your ego wants stuff that it believes will keep you safe and attractive. Cut to: the entire basis of the advertising industry. "Buy this, and you will be rich (ego hears: have lots of food and status), attractive (ego hears:

able to procreate and be included in the safety of the tribe) and power-ful (ego hears: more attractive than others, thus ensuring survival and procreation).

It might be tempting to vilify the ego, but it's just as appropriate to offer the ego immense gratitude for the great job it's doing keeping us safe. The problem is that it's also, paradoxically, killing us. It's suppressing the expression of life that calls to us from the spirit. The spirit calls, "This is who I crave to be!" and the ego responds, "Are you crazy??!!! That's *way* too risky!! People might disapprove and think you're different and weird. Just lay low and play along like everybody else, or we're gonna get our head chopped off."

ACTION

Ask yourself: "Where do I play small in life, hold myself back from my potential, for fear of being rejected?" Think about that question in terms of your work life and your relationships. Our greatest fears are that we are "not good enough," and that we won't be loved. We all live with these deep-seated fears. How aware are you of the way these fears play into your life?

Then there's the spirit. I'm not referencing any religion or particular spiritual tradition here—bring to this concept whatever is true for you. I'm just pointing to this force within us that holds a knowing about who we are, what matters most, what we are here to create, and what wants to be expressed through us.

Our spirit is a creative life force within us that has embedded in it the "DNA" of our unique desire. It's fundamental to what differentiates us from others, yet it's also the thing linking us to all of life and humanity.

Ultimately, life is a dance between the wants of the ego and the yearning of the spirit. The spirit wants to be free and express itself, while the ego wants to ensure its survival.

Our job is to listen to what our spirit says it needs to be fully expressed and alive, to distinguish its call from the ego's call, and to courageously answer to our spirit: YES! Let's do it! And then to bring a whole lot of compassion to ourselves as we struggle to make it so. Occasionally, we need to just thank our overzealous ego for its good intention, even if we know that we don't need all the protection it thinks we do. All that safety is taking way too big a toll on us—it is robbing us of our aliveness, our life force.

What's the easiest way to tell the difference between the call of the spirit and the call of the ego?

1. When you feel a desire, repeatedly ask yourself, as we did in the previous exercise, "and that would bring me…" until you get to "the end." If the ultimate answer is about security and belonging, and being loved, safe, attractive, fed, etc., then you are likely looking at the call of the ego. If the ultimate answer has to do with aliveness, creativity, compassion, or love, then you are likely hearing the call of your spirit.

2. Look for "resonance" and learn to distinguish it from "dissonance." Resonance is a feeling of harmony, goodness, energy and purpose inside you—like a pretty musical chord. Dissonance is the feeling of unease, lifelessness, worry or wrongness in you—like an ugly musical chord. The call of the spirit tends to induce resonance (though it can also cause fear). It's exciting. The call of the ego tends to come with a dissonant feeling (because deep down your spirit knows that it wants its way, and the ego is suppressing its

expression). Your spirit tends to communicate what will go right and feel good about something, while your ego warns you about what could go wrong.

Why does all of this matter? Because of all the wealthy people I know, only those who are honoring their spirit are happy. Those who are focused on mainly feeding their ego are slogging along a tiring, fruitless, desperate and stressful path. Or simply living an "OK" life.

Security and Aliveness

When you get down to it, there are two feelings we most want in life: security and aliveness. And what do you know? Our spirit most craves aliveness, whereas our ego most craves security. And embedded in virtually everything having to do with our money is the hope that the end result will be **aliveness, security or both**.

Bringing it to Life

There you have it. That's my take on life. That's wealth. That's Woohoo! It's the sound your spirit makes when you say "Yes!" to it, and it gets to express itself through you. Wealth is the same thing. Wealth and Woohoo! are both about aliveness and choosing to honor your spirit. Wealth is having Woohoo!

We've started this book, in part, by looking at the WHY of wealth. Why become wealthy? Because it's your deepest yearning. It may well be your only mission in life. Not to accumulate money, but rather **to be your best, to give your best, to burn your brightest and to be brilliant about how you use money to amplify yourself and your life.**

CHAPTER 4

The 7 Pillars of Woohoo! Wealth

So let's get to it…

Why am I not wealthy? Where's my Woohoo! Wealth?

I'm talking with a guy named Mike. Mike's intrigued about creating wealth. He believes he'll be wealthy someday, but would love to know more about why people do or don't become wealthy. Mike works a job that he doesn't especially love, though he doesn't hate it. His finances are pretty rough—he's barely got anything saved and spends most of his income. Mike hears about the work I do and asks the fundamental question: "Why am I not wealthy?"

So I ask him seven questions:

1. "Mike—are you really committed to becoming wealthy?"

   "Well, I guess, yeah. I want to be wealthy. What do you mean by committed?"

2. "What do you really most want in life?"

   "Um…"

3. "What's blocking you from building wealth? What internal or external obstacles are you facing?"

"I'm not sure—that's what I'm asking you."

4. "What's your net worth, your cash flow, the cost of the lifestyle you want and the amount you need saved to fund it forever?"

"Uh… I'm not sure."

5. "What's your specific game plan for building the assets you want to support your lifestyle? How will you accumulate wealth?"

"I'm not sure. Keep working my job and get raises, I guess."

6. "Who's helping you become wealthy?"

"What do you mean helping me? You mean like my CPA?"

7. "What's holding you back from going for it?"

"Going for what?"

Having allowed him to fall into the trap, I respond…

"OK, Mike. Here's your answer. Here are the seven reasons you aren't wealthy:"

1. You aren't in the game of creating wealth.
2. You don't know what you want.
3. You don't know your obstacles or have a plan to deal with them.
4. You don't know your own numbers.
5. You don't have a specific wealth-building plan.
6. You aren't getting the help you need to succeed.
7. You are afraid.

"Yeah, maybe, but I'm still pretty sure I'm gonna be wealthy." He concludes.

(By the way, Mike doesn't exist—this is just a mashup of all the conversations like this I've had.)

In all these years of observing people who are wealthy and happy, and of searching for common factors that distinguish them from those who are neither wealthy nor especially happy, I've been able to identify numerous differences. And I've boiled them down for this book to seven key differences.

One way to look at it is by asking: why am I not wealthier and happier? Mike illustrated those reasons for us.

The other way to look at it is to ask this:

What are the pillars of wealth? What have the wealthy done right? What are they doing that we can also do to create wealth? These are the inverse of what Mike's got going on.

Here we have it:

The 7 Pillars of Woohoo! Wealth

The seven magical, mystical, ancient and powerful KEYS to creating Woohoo! Wealth:

1. Get in the game—commit to creating wealth.
2. Know what you want.
3. Know your obstacles.
4. Know your numbers.
5. Have a specific wealth-building plan.
6. Get help.
7. Be courageous.

This is going to serve as our framework, our formula, our system for building Woohoo! Wealth. Each chapter in this section will take one of the seven pillars and cover: What the pillar is, why it is important, what the problem is if overlooked, and what you should do to ensure you have this in place.

You can think of these pillars as supporting the structure of wealth. Missing pillars are always a threat to the stability of a structure. The same is true here. Every pillar is essential to success in building Woohoo! Wealth.

CHAPTER 5

Pillar #1: Get In The Game And Play To Win

If you want to be wealthy, you've got to get in the game. You must be **actively dedicated to creating wealth**. It's not just going to happen. You can do all the affirmations you want and rely on the "law of attraction" all you want—it won't work if you aren't in the game.

Most people want to be wealthy and happy. Further, most people believe that they *are* in the game, yet really aren't!

Why is that a problem? Think about it—where in life do you regularly attain your wishes, goals, or dreams without really being actively engaged in the game of realizing them, without having clarity about what you want, what it's going to take to get that, and a specific plan for achieving it?

Let's take weight loss as an example. What's the difference between people who radiate excitement as they show you before and after pictures proving they lost 75 pounds and those who didn't? One huge difference is that the people who lost weight were in the game! You could tell they were, because they were taking smart and decisive action in the areas of nutrition and exercise.

There's a huge difference between wanting something and creating something. Most people want wealth and well-being, and yet really aren't in the game. They don't know the rules, don't know how to keep score, aren't bringing energy, passion and dedication to the pursuit, and aren't enjoying the game. They feel hopeless.

What are some of the signs that you ARE or AREN'T in various games? Let's take the game of getting physically fit for example…

Signs you **aren't** in the game:

- You aren't fit.
- You are not fitter than you were a month or a year ago.
- You aren't lifting a weight, swimming a lap, climbing a hill, or running a trail, and haven't in quite a while.
- You've got good reasons why you haven't been able to.
- Your fitness is frustrating you.
- You're going it alone—you have no training, support, or accountability partners.

Now, let's look at signs you **are** in the game of getting fit:

- You worked out today. And yesterday. And you will tomorrow.
- You enjoyed it, because you chose an exercise you *want* to do.
- You've got specific fitness goals (e.g., body weight, lap time, etc.) and you are seeing (even charting) your progress towards them.
- Your success is fueling additional energy for the game.
- You have support in the form of friends with whom you work out, or a trainer, or a fitness program.
- You are fitter than you were before, and you are confident you will be more fit in the future, because you know what you want, have a plan, are implementing it, and it's working.

When you are IN the game, there are many signs telling you that. Now, when it comes to building wealth and well-being, are you in the game?

ACTION

Take a moment to look for signs in your life that would give you clues as to whether you are officially in the game of building wealth and thriving, and that you are playing to win. Get a sheet of paper and make one column entitled, "In the Game," and another column entitled, "Watching the Game."

Now, look at your life and ask yourself: "What evidence do I see that I am committed to creating wealth?" Write down evidence such as "I'm saving 15% of my income" in the In the Game column. Write down evidence such as "I haven't opened a bank statement in two years" in the Watching the Game column.

Don't forget to look at the outer world (action, strategy, plans, bank accounts, etc.) and the inner world (commitment, clarity, energy, drive, courage, optimism, etc.) to look for clues. Got it? Go.

OK. What conclusion might you draw from this exercise? Are you IN and playing to WIN? Or are you mainly hoping to be wealthy someday? Was it hard to know what evidence to seek?

If you are already a multi-millionaire, do you love your life? Are you in the game of creating a life you love, or mainly hoping that someday you'll love it? Or are you just accepting "a pretty good life"?

Here are some signs that you are *not* in the game of building wealth and well-being:

1. It took you a while to do that exercise (signifying that you are unclear about whether or not you are in). If the exercise had been "signs you love your kids," you wouldn't even need to start—you would just know that you love your kids. When you are in the game of wealth building, you are crystal clear about it.

2. You don't have a really clear and vivid picture about what you most want in life, of what true wealth is for you.

3. You aren't clear about the internal obstacles you face in building wealth.

4. You don't know your numbers: what your ideal life costs are, what asset base you need to support that, or where you stand today in terms of net worth and cash flow.

5. You don't have a specific plan for exactly how you are going to build wealth or what asset-building method you will use.

6. You don't have help, guidance or support.

7. You're afraid to go for what you want in life.

Here, on the other hand, are signs that you are IN and playing to WIN the game of creating wealth and well-being . .

1. You have a conscious **commitment** to building the wealth and happiness you want in life. Like getting fit—you know you are in the game, because you have decided to play it and see evidence that you are in it; evidence like…

2. You have an energizing and vivid **vision of what you really want in life**, of what's most important to you, and of what life well-lived on your terms looks and feels like. This vision has been created from your spirit rather than from your "ego," and you are confident that it is fulfilling. It's your Woohoo!, and you are clear about what part of it money can buy and what part has little to do with money.

3. You're really clear about how your brain wiring and programming, and your daily actions can **inhibit or facilitate** building wealth.

4. You **know your numbers**: where you stand financially today, what your ideal life costs are, and how much wealth is required to support that forever.

5. You have a **specific plan for building the required wealth** (and this plan doesn't involve you hating your work and life until you are "free").

6. You've got the **support** you need to accelerate your success.

7. You are being **courageous**—frequently feeling fear and acting in spite of it.

Nope, it's not a coincidence that the seven signs of being in the game of wealth are the seven pillars as well. Woohoo!

How?

OK. So, how do you GET IN THE GAME and PLAY TO WIN?

Decide.

Yup—that's it. Just say, "I'm in. Game on."

Everything starts with a decision. The Latin origin of the word *decide* means to cut off all other possibilities. That's what deciding does for you—it makes all other options non-options.

But wait—that's kind of anti-climactic isn't it? Well, OK. If you want, you can dramatically skid into financial Armageddon, losing your house and family, only to finally declare to the universe, "Enough! I must finally do something about this now!!!" Wait for drama if you need it.

But really, I believe that it's like getting fit. Sometimes, you just start by *deciding* you are going to go to the gym. And you go, and it feels good, you get the result you wanted, and you go back again. And the energy builds on itself. And before you know it, you are a person who is fit, and it's just who you are now.

It's the same with getting into the game of thriving wealth—just say, "I'm game—let's do it. I want that." And then *take the next step* (which in this case means going on to pillar #2). Commit and prove your commitment by taking step 2. That's it.

If you feel like you are already somewhat in the game, decide to *up your game!*

And here's the cool part. The energy and passion will come. Specifically, you will find it in the second pillar of wealth: knowing what you really want. For now, just decide to really start and then bring a willingness and curiosity.

When I was a boy, we were on a trip on the coast of England, and a food truck was selling French fries. Much to my chagrin, the fry guy was pouring vinegar on the fries. What? Ruin perfectly good fries? My parents urged me to just try it. No way. After much coaxing, I finally did. And I've rarely had fries *without* vinegar since. The point? Just say *yes* to get in the game of creating wealth, and you are likely to never want to be out of it again. You'll see. Just try it!

Imagine standing in a group of people with a leader asking: "Who's ready to thrive?" and everybody raises a hand. "Who's ready to dive in and get started right now?" Raise your hand again. Decide that you are IN. That's the difference between a want and a commitment. Commitment takes your wanting and converts it to action, *now*.

And here's a really important point. In deciding, you are officially saying: I'm not going to rely on luck; I'm going to make it happen through being informed, committed, taking focused action and persevering. I'll take any luck that comes my way, but luck is not my game plan. Hope is not my strategy.

Most people *think* they are committed to building wealth ("well I'm working; I'm earning money; I'm saving a little, aren't I? I *want* to be rich!") yet frankly are just wandering around on the field without a goal, and without knowing the rules and the obstacles. The first pillar of wealth is to simply *decide* to play the game with heart, and stick around long enough to learn the rules, start playing the game intelligently, and get energized by it. You'll love it and want to keep playing—playing to win.

Finally, I believe this is our JOB in life. This IS life: learning how to thrive, how to be alive, and how to create the wealth to support and fuel us.

ACTION

Option 1: Stand up and declare out loud: "Game on! I'm in! Show me the Money! Show me the LIFE!"

Option 2: If option 1 isn't enough, and you want to start with a little more drama and an even bigger commitment to building wealth, try this visualization exercise:

Take a good look at the ways in which you are floundering at building the wealth and the life you want. Be straight with yourself. Are you on track? Do you have a game plan? Are you thriving in life? If your answers are mostly negative, good (for this Action). I want you to imagine that you keep on keeping on with whatever you are doing. Forever. Imagine yourself NEVER thriving. Imagine your life just OK for the rest of your life. Imagine never having the money to do the things you most yearn to do. Imagine never really having radiant energy and fulfilled happiness. See your life with a grey tone cast over it. Really vividly imagine it. See how this plays out in your relationships and in your health. What toll does this take on you? Allow yourself to feel pathetic about it. See this extending five years into your future. Picture it. What impact has this had on your life? See it going ten years, even twenty years. See it going until your death. Imagine that this is the life to which you are condemned. Picture it mediocre at best, pathetic or even tragic at worst. Picture what you have left of friends and family gathered around your grave without a great deal to say about your life. Allow yourself to go here and feel the pain of what your life could be like. Taste the pain of it. Let yourself feel it.

ACTION, continued

Once, and only once, you can feel that pain, decide what you want to do about it. Now, might you want to decide to commit to building Woohoo! Wealth? Sometimes, we have to feel enough pain to want to change. Feel that pain and then use it to choose a different life for yourself.

CHAPTER 6

Pillar #2: Know What You Really Want

If I were asked, "What's the *single* most important thing you can do to build true wealth?" I would answer: Know what you most deeply want.

Most people really don't know what they want in life.

What does happiness look like for them? Who do they want to be? What is the impact they want to have on the world? What is their purpose and passion? What are their gifts to give?

Why is that a problem? Because when you don't know what you want, you usually don't get it. And when what you want is driven by outside forces (society, culture, family, consumerism, advertisers), then you are playing the game to lose—you won't make yourself happy, and you won't make others happy either. You won't thrive. You'll have little Woohoo! It's a game you just can't win. You'll have missed the ultimate opportunity in life—to really live it and love it.

ACTION

Give yourself just fifteen seconds to answer this question:

What do you really want?

Now stop. The telltale sign is this: Did you have to stop and think about it? Start to form your ideas? Ponder a bit? Start to squint to see through the fog? Or were you able to draw a vivid vision of what's most important to you, of what you really want most in life? A vision that encompasses the whole of your life: relationships, finance, health, creativity, career, etc.?

With clarity about what you want, you can chart a course towards it and constantly make adjustments along the way. Without clarity, with just a vague sense or abstract concept of what you want, you are essentially drifting, with low probability of success.

And again, without distinguishing between the wants of your ego and the wants of your spirit, you'll misdirect a lot of time and energy pursuing things with low return on effort. The things our ego craves satisfy us temporarily, but don't fulfill us.

Figuring Out What You Really Want

My teacher and colleague, George Kinder, is known in the financial planning community as the Father of Life Planning. You might think of life planning as financial planning meets life coaching. George was a pioneer in prodding the profession to look beyond just organizing clients' finances, in order to help people discover, clarify, pursue and attain what they really want in life. They don't want organized finances—they only hope those will serve as a means to what they ultimately want: freedom, however they define it.

The Three Questions

George is well known for his Three Questions. In my years of working with clients, I've found that the Three Questions are just about the quickest way to get to the heart of what you really want, what matters most to you. They powerfully reveal what's most important in your life, what you want it to be all about. So you're going to answer the Three Questions.

Believe it or not, this could be a turning point in your life. It certainly was for me. Answering these questions led me to quit my job, take eighteen months off, travel the world with my wife and two kids, deepen my training in coaching and leadership, to spend tons of time in nature and in the ocean, with friends and family, and ultimately to redefine my career and start my own wealth management firm and wealth training company.

Just those three little questions! They have changed many, many lives. As an exercise, you too will answer these questions. I invite you to approach this exercise as though it has the same potential for you. How might you do that?

First, really do this. Don't just read it. Set aside a good hour or more during which you'll have peace and quiet, be in an environment you love, have energy, and allow yourself to really reflect. This is not something you do while the kids need your attention or while periodically checking email or sports scores.

Second, please only read one question at a time and answer it before even reading the next question. In other words, don't read ahead. Answer Question #1, and only after you are done, go on to Question #2. It works better that way, and you'll only be cheating yourself by reading ahead.

Third, give yourself permission to really dream, to really reflect, and to really feel. You are taking time to take stock of what you really want in life, what's really important to you. Give it your all, and enjoy it. Let yourself go. Have fun.

You won't get much from just quickly reading the question and coming up with a few quick answers. The power of this exercise comes from taking the time to slow down and access your deeper answers.

When you are ready, turn the page to Question 1 and settle in to reflect, dream and answer. Only when you are done, turn the page to Question #2 and answer it. Again, once finished with Question #2, please move on to Question #3.

So, please stop reading now, until you are ready to answer the questions, and you know you'll have the time for them.

"Hold fast to dreams, for if dreams die, life is a broken winged bird that cannot fly."

Langston Hughes

OK. Go ahead…

Question #1

I want you to imagine that you are financially secure, that you have enough money to take care of your needs, now and in the future. Imagine that you have all the money you could want.

The question is: With this complete financial freedom, how would you live your life? What would you change? Let yourself go. Really imagine. Don't hold back on your dreams.

Describe a life that is complete, one that is richly yours.

This material was developed by George Kinder and the Kinder Institute of Life Planning. It is used by financial planning professionals who hold the Registered Life Planner® (RLP®) designation. A directory of Registered Life Planners is available at **www.kinderinstitute.com/dir**. Used here by permission of George Kinder © 2006.

Question #2

This time you visit your doctor, who tells you that you have only 5–10 years left to live. The good part is that you won't ever feel sick. The bad news is that you will have no notice of the moment of your death.

What will you do in the time you have remaining to live? Will you change your life, and how will you do it?

(Do you still have the money from Question #1, or not? Answer whichever way is more poignant for you.)

This material was developed by George Kinder and the Kinder Institute of Life Planning. It is used by financial planning professionals who hold the Registered Life Planner® (RLP®) designation. A directory of Registered Life Planners is available at **www.kinderinstitute.com/dir**. Used here by permission of George Kinder © 2006.

Question #3

This time your doctor shocks you with the news that you have only one day left to live. Your time on the planet is over. Notice what feelings arise as you confront your very real mortality.

Ask yourself:

What did I miss? Who did I not get to be? What did I not get to do?

This material was developed by George Kinder and the Kinder Institute of Life Planning. It is used by financial planning professionals who hold the Registered Life Planner® (RLP®) designation. A directory of Registered Life Planners is available at www.kinderinstitute.com/dir. Used here by permission of George Kinder © 2006.

Welcome back, and well done! How was that?

You've just answered the Three Questions and are likely feeling some emotion about it, some resonance, and experiencing a heightened clarity about what's important to you in life.

A little aside… read this if you didn't actually answer the question:

> If you didn't answer the questions, I have a request. Jump in! What the hell—what've you got to lose? Read this book like you mean it. Start like your life depends on it. Because you know what? It does! The way you read this book is the way you do anything in life. You've picked up a book called *Woohoo! Wealth* and you're no doubt looking for heavy doses of both of those things. I promise you won't get them reading passively, *considering* the exercises instead of *doing* them. That would be like going to the gym and looking at the workout machines, seeing how they work, and believing you will get fit by observing. You've got to sit down at the machine and push.
>
> If you aren't going to do the work, put the book down and come back another day when you are genuinely ready to play— you've already found the answer to why you aren't wealthy and/ or don't have Woohoo! It's because you aren't *in* the game. You're *watching* it.

What's the heart of it?

OK. So, you've answered the Three Questions. Now let's deepen and distill that.

ACTION

Now read back over your answers, and as you do so, try to draw out the essence of what's most important to you by applying some or all of these questions:

- What are the 3–5 most important themes, ideas or wishes I came up with?
- What's the one most important thing?
- As I read, when do I feel most emotion—sadness, joy, hope or excitement? (Pay attention to that. What's the emotion about?)
- What's my "secret sorrow?"—the sadness I feel about something unfulfilled in my life?
- What desire is my soul or spirit expressing here?
- If my inner mental "gremlin" were to take a lunch break, and really leave me completely free and vulnerable to dream and truly say what I most want, what would I say?
- What do I really want?
- Pay particular attention to your answers from Question #3. What's it telling you?
- Now, imagine that you were going to be granted whatever you wish for next, with certainty. Based on all of what you just wrote, read, and reflected upon, what is it that you really want? Go ahead—wish for it. Say what you want. Write it down. Declare it.
- If you knew that you had the unconditional support and approval of everyone around you, what would you allow yourself? What would you do or begin.
- If you knew you would not fail, what would you try?
- What is it you really need to have, to be, and to do for your life to feel complete, authentic and alive—to have Woohoo!?

Keep going—try to distill it down to its essence. What do you really want!? Is it to slow down or speed up? Is it to create more, professionally, or to scale back to be home with the kids? Is it to express yourself artistically?

> ### ACTION, continued
>
> To strengthen your health? Is it to run your own business? Is it to spend time volunteering in Africa? What's the life you want to live? What must you have, do or be in your life for it to feel complete and fulfilled?
>
> Have fun with it, or get angry about it, or get inspired about it. Try getting into different postures, or into different rooms or spaces, to help you shift your energy and perspective to try to draw out the golden nuggets.
>
> Write it down. Summarize on paper what you have seen and learned from doing this exercise.

Wonderful.

At this point, you may be experiencing a newfound level of clarity and energy. That's the power of going in and going deep for answers, and having the courage to ask and listen. If so, wonderful; you have tapped a new energy source and found a compass heading. Isn't it awesome? Congratulations—you're "finding your way home."

We'll take next steps with your answers shortly.

"The pain pushes you until your vision pulls you."
Michael Bernard Beckwith

What's It All About?

I now want to share with you what life planners around the world have found to be the most common themes in the answers to the Three Questions. The same answers repeatedly surface to the top of people's greatest wishes, and illustrate what people find most important in life. These might not all resonate with you—they are just the most common.

Here are the top five:

1. **Family**: At the end of the day, when faced with our mortality, we most quickly come to see our family as the most important thing in our life. We crave meaningful relationships, closeness, presence, healing and the expression of love.

2. **Spirit**: We yearn to feel connected to our higher selves, to a universal spirit, and to be connected to meaning and purpose. This can take the form of religion but it needn't. We want a connection with the biggest picture, to feel inspired by it and to feel a part of it. We want to seek and find our own answers to "What's it all about?"

3. **Creativity**: Most people have a deep yearning to create, build, and contribute. Another way of framing creativity is the desire to use one's gifts to put something meaningful and/or beautiful into the world. People are often surprised to see creativity so high on the list, yet our creative impulse is extremely strong. Perhaps embedded in our desire to create is also our desire to matter.

4. **Community**: Beyond family, we yearn to be connected to a community of friends, associates, neighbors, or countrymen. We want to feel part of and connected with our brothers and sisters. We want to be in our tribe.

5. **Sense of Place:** We have a strong desire to live in a particular environment, whether physical (e.g., the coast) or ideological (e.g., spiritual community). We feel connected to special homes, land, buildings, and atmospheres. This is the "water we swim in," and people have strong desires for particular environments and places. This can extend to caring for the planet and the environment as a whole.

Through these top five answers, people are fundamentally declaring, "I want to be a loving and creative person deeply connected with and impacting my family, friends, community and environment."

What we most want, our deepest desire, is to really live. To be truly, fully, magnificently alive! These are the five areas through which most people will access their aliveness. Soon, we'll look at exactly how to do that.

Something else I've seen as a common theme has been the desire to slow things down. When people describe the life they want, they typically describe a pace that is slower than the lives they are now leading and more focused on the top five things above. People want slower, simpler, more intentional and meaningful living. And we want to more deeply honor our own calling rather than other people's expectations of us.

ACTION

How about for you? Go back over your answers to the Three Questions and see where your answers fall in these five categories.

When I went through the three questions the first time (sure—you can redo these forever and continue to deepen your clarity and vision), there were a couple of really core yearnings I had. The third question really illuminated my greatest regret in life to that point: that I'd never really found and used my "voice" (not as in singing voice, but as in having an authentic message and the courage to speak it). I was moved to tears by the pain and frustration of that. Also, I yearned for more time with my young children and wife—I just felt so sad about having to be away from them so much. Also, I wanted to spend more time surfing in the ocean (which, though you may laugh, most surfers consider a spiritual activity). I also wanted to slow down and be in control of how I design my days. There were a few things in the category of "stuff" that I wanted, but most of what I discovered was about the person I wanted be, the creativity I wanted to put into the world, and the freedom I wanted to enjoy.

I've made all these things real in my life as a result of asking what I really wanted and following the further steps we'll get into. I took time off, and our family embarked on a four-month adventure. From RV-ing through Glacier, Yellowstone and Grand Teton National parks, to canoe-tripping in the remote Canadian wilderness, and from watching the Highland Games in Scotland to rejuvenating in Provence, my family and I spent tons of time together. I surf and hike all the time. I run my own business, in which I "use my voice," and enjoy lots of freedom and free time. The point is, I got clear about what's most important to me and decided to make it happen.

Remember how, in the first step, I noted that there might not be a lot of energy in the decision to "get in the game." Well, once you connect with what you really want—when you allow yourself to entertain the hope that you might actually get that—you'll tap a huge energy source. That energy comes from being optimistic that you can have what you most deeply want, of being on *your* path. It's your *reason* for taking action and building wealth.

I just guided a couple, Al and Kim, through the Three Questions the other day. What do they most want?
- To live slowly.
- To share their life experience and wisdom with their children as their legacy.
- To awaken with gratitude, and end the day likewise.
- To eat simple, delicious, organic food.
- To help leaders in business and community achieve their next level of success.

- To inspire others to live in line with their core values.
- To have the courage to buck convention and to live by their own rules.

Or Janine: what does she most want?
- To have a child.
- To lead a team of dynamic thinkers to creatively solve entrepreneurial challenges.

Or Elise:
- To reconnect with her husband.
- To heal her relationship with her sister.
- To spend a year traveling with her family.

Or Simon:
- To leave his dry, technology consulting work to teach kids science.
- To have more fun!

What about you? What did you come up with?

The Best Things in Life Are...

Did you notice something wonderful in reviewing your answers?

Most of the things that we want the *very* most really aren't about money, and they usually don't require a great deal of it.

Seldom do material things rank very highly on people's lists. I have yet to see that someone's greatest life regret is never having bought a Lamborghini. Especially when facing the end of life, people tend not to care too much about possessions. It tends to come down to regrets about not having been more alive, regrets about having played it too safe or regrets about having just gone through the motions without ever finding a passionate way to live.

Sure, money touches most things in life. You might, for example, need to buy a plane ticket to go visit mom, but it doesn't cost money to express your love for her and to let her know how grateful you are that she's done her very best for you. And we usually have flexibility in how much money it costs—you can still *call* mom to tell her if you can't afford the ticket. Dining with friends costs money, but you can also find less expensive ways of connecting, such as going for a hike together or hosting a potluck.

I just watched a video clip in which someone with a terminal cancer has his final weeks of life documented. Paradoxically, he is brought alive by the experience, finally free of the fear of death, because of its imminent certainty. And he's energized. Of all the things he can choose to say, he finds nothing more important than expressing his love for his wife and two daughters. I find these lessons from the end of a life very powerful.

How might you be set free to really live if you knew you were going to die? If you were being documented, and had to sum it all up for the camera, what would you have to say?

That also reminds me of another story: I was on my morning walk when I came across my friend Dave. He's a big, wonderful, loving auto detailer. He spends his week washing cars and his weekends running a ministry in his neighborhood of Marin City, an island of financial under-privilege in the affluent sea that is Marin County, CA. Every time Dave sees me, he makes a point of greeting me smiling, saying he loves me, acknowledging what a good man and father I am and asking after my children and wife. And he means it. He grew up troubled, and turned his life around. He organized the feeding of 3,000 families last Thanksgiving. That's the kind of guy he is.

This morning, he told me of detailing a Ferrari for a man with a net worth of over $100 million. This man, like our previous guy from the video, is also on his deathbed, and asked to have Dave brought into his room. And in one of his last acts of life, this man of riches and privilege asked his auto detailer for the secret to happiness. There you have it— the "rich" man asking the "poor" man for the secret to "true" wealth. Beautiful. I couldn't have made up a better story.

Another story: I had lunch with a good friend, Tim, whose family friend, Susan, called him for financial advice. She dumped all her statements on him to get his take. She said things like, "I mean, look at this account worth fifty—I think it should be a hundred! Right? Don't you?" Tim suggested to her that she hire a financial adviser. He offered her a number of names, including mine. He noted that one thing I do is help people get clear about what it is they want and how to align their financial lives with that. She replied, "If I don't know what I want in my life by now, I'm in big trouble!" The trouble I saw was this: Her account of $50, which she thought should be $100… we're talking *million*. This is a woman with a net worth of $250 million, and she's counting her chips and feeling that they should be double. No doubt if *you* had that $250 million, you would feel abundance, right? She probably thought she would too.

"The only wealth which you will keep forever is the wealth you have given away."

Marcus Aurelius

A Special Form of Wealth

When we look back at the top five answers for what we most deeply want in life, we see that the things we most want in life are a special form of wealth. Unlike a limited resource which is depleted as you give more and more of it away, a lot of what we most want has a magical quality: the more you give, the more you have. Giving does not deplete your supply, and usually increases it.

For example, when you express love for your family, you have just as much as before you expressed it, and you are likely to experience more (within yourself for having expressed it, and from your family in return—except from that crotchety old bastard Uncle Joe!). When you want to live with integrity, doing so doesn't deplete your integrity—it bolsters it and inspires it in others. When you create, you aren't left with less creativity. When you are generous with your attention for your children, you haven't depleted your supply of attention.

One of the most important points that I can make is this: Our path to Woohoo! Wealth has lots to do with recognizing that the most important things in our lives aren't things, and **what we most want in life, the *really* important stuff, is most likely accessible without large quantities of money**.

And that's GREAT news (or at least a great reminder).

Why is this so important? Because one of our great fears is this: "I'm afraid that I won't have enough money and won't be able to buy and do the stuff I want, and then I'll be deprived of the important things in life and die miserable and dejected." We all have some form of this fear in us. It's really hard to live in modern American society without having had this belief planted in us. When we see advertised every day that our joy and security in life will come from having money, stuff, status and power, then, by extension, the message is that without those we will be unhappy and insecure.

I know this is simplifying or stating the obvious in certain ways, yet the path to creating wealth has a crucial element: defining wealth for *yourself*. That's what the Three Questions are designed to do. And I'm *certain* that the vision of wealth you just created for yourself is *extremely* different from what Madison Avenue has created for you.

I state the obvious because perhaps it's not so obvious. Clichés have a way of discouraging us from considering their deeper truth, because they are trite. "Money can't buy happiness," "The best things in life aren't things," or "The best things in life are free." As soon as we hear that, our brain shuts down, because "we already know that," and it has nothing further to gain by considering it more deeply.

Yet too often, when our lives are examined, we are living in contradiction to what we know to be true. We *know what to do*, but do we *do what we know?*" We often seek more "stuff" in the quest to be happier. Why would we do that when we already know it doesn't work?

In any case, right now the good news should be this:

1. You are much clearer about what you want.
2. You are inspired and energized by it.
3. You are relieved to see that most of what you want in life really isn't about the money, though you recognize money touches it all.

When can I have it?

ACTION

Now try this one on for size: look at the list of what you most want. How much of that is available to you right now, without money (or with little impact from money)? For example, "to slow down and live more appreciatively" or "to reconnect with my husband" or "to have the courage to speak my mind" or "to take better care of my health." What are the things on your list that have more to do with your intention than your wallet? Circle those.

Now look at the items that clearly require money, and underline those.

ACTION, continued

Examples would be: "a larger home in the next neighborhood" or "to travel to India" or "to have the freedom to be a stay-at-home mother." Underline those.

A crucial part of Woohoo! Wealth planning is distinguishing what we're planning for *financially* versus what we're planning for more *personally* or *internally*.

I hope that at this point in the book, your perspective has shifted. Most people who wonder why they aren't wealthier are effectively wondering why they don't have more money. By now, you should see that **the number one obstacle to wealth is simply not being clear about what wealth is for you**. Rather than a clear, moving and inspiring vision, you have fog or someone else's vision in your brain.

And once you know what you want, you begin to see that most of it doesn't take tons of money, and that lots of it is accessible to you right now. You've just done something magical: you've moved "wealth" much closer to you. The finish line just got closer. How about *that* for shortening the journey to wealth?

Fear not—the latter part of this book is all about real money in the real world, and how to create monetary wealth. I'm not living in a fantasy world—I know that you want and need real money. We'll get strategic about that. We've started here because it makes that job easier: you end up needing a lot less money when you've clarified what actually *does* bring you fulfillment in life. And you end up with a lot more drive and energy to get the money you want, because *why* you want it matters so deeply to you.

I enjoy a great lifestyle and want to maintain it forever. I love enjoying the finest things in life. I wish loads of money on you, myself and everyone so that we may have the financial freedom to enjoy the great things the world has to offer. I just want us to have our priorities straight.

Getting More Vivid and Specific

Which sounds better to you:

1. A great vacation.
2. A great vacation in Kauai for over a week. Great seafood and ripe fruit. Rental car included.
3. A ten-day trip to the north coast of Kauai, staying in a beachfront, five-bedroom house to the left of the pier, with cook, maid, and convertible Jeep Wrangler rental car. Fresh mahi mahi and ripe mangos, warm sand and refreshing 72-degree water.

Yup, it's #3. Our brain has a much easier time getting energized and excited about detailed, specific images that it can imagine seeing, touching, tasting, smelling, and hearing. Remember how I claimed that virtually everything we do in life is in search of a feeling? Our brain gets most excited when it can imagine feeling that feeling.

We want wealth and happiness. Who doesn't? But which is more exciting for you: "lots of money" or "$15 million"? "Seeing your best friend more often" or "a weekly, Thursday-night dinner with your best friend trying out various ethnic cuisines in the city"?

You get the point: we draw energy from clarity and specificity. **Abstractions only light us up so much.** To milk them, we need to get more specific.

"Knowledge of what is possible is the beginning of happiness."
George Santayana

In light of that, our job now is to take your answers from the Three Questions (which are often abstract) and get more specific and vivid with them.

> "We lift ourselves by our thought. We climb upon our vision of ourselves. If you want to enlarge your life, you must first enlarge your thought of it and of yourself. Hold the ideal of yourself as you long to be, always everywhere."
>
> **Orison Swett Marden**

This One Goes to 11!

Remember how we started with the Woohoo! Wealth graph, and you drew an arrow from where you are to where you want to be? Well, all this work so far has been about moving upward on the graph and defining point B. You are painting the picture of the life you want. Like a ship charting its course, you are getting clear about your current position and your destination.

ACTION

In this exercise, we're going to draw a more vivid picture of what you most want in various specific areas of your life.

Take a look at the categories below:
- Career/Mission
- Finances
- Health/Fitness/Body
- Friends & Family
- Significant Other/Romance
- Personal Growth
- Fun & Recreation

ACTION, continued

- Physical Environment
- Creativity
- Community
- Time

Use these life categories, and feel free to add any others important to you or to skip any.

Take out a sheet of paper and write down the various areas of life you want to consider.

Now, for each area of life, ask yourself **specifically** what that area would look like if you rated it a 10 (on a scale of 1 to 10). Better yet, if you rated it an 11! Close your eyes; picture it; feel it.

For example, in the area of health, create a vivid picture of how your health would feel, how your body would feel, and how your fitness level would feel and look. What does your doctor say about your health? What's your weight? How many miles can you run? Get detailed and specific and inspired. What would be awesome?

Do that for each area of your life. You are painting the picture of what you most want in life and making it more specific and vivid. Write it down.

Also, keep in mind that the question "how will I do it?" can snuff your dreams just as they are emerging. For example, "I would love to lead wilderness adventures" is a vision that can easily be crushed with questions and fears about "how" you could make a living at it, "how" you can do that with young kids, "how" you can do that when you are overweight, etc. Something absolutely key to dreaming and getting in touch with what matters to you, is giving yourself the freedom not to have the answers to "how" yet. Your job is to build your connection to and excitement about what matters to you. And you'll find that the how tends to present itself when you commit to something deeply meaningful.

Note that another powerful way to do this exercise is using what's called a vision board. Think of it as a big bulletin board on which you post images, words, quotes, fabrics, objects—anything, really. The idea is to collect something visual and tangible that inspires you and illustrates what you want. The part of us that dreams of what we want thinks in images. So feel free to use images to help it. **www.Pinterest.com** is a website that allows you to create these kinds of collections of images (and share them with other Pinterest users). It's also a great place to *find* the images. Check it out.

And don't underestimate the power of this exercise. This is an extremely important thing you are doing: painting the picture of what you most want in life. If you don't do it here, when *are* you going to do it? What else do you have going on more important than figuring this out? You may have more *pressing* things demanding your attention, but what could be more important than this—designing your life?!

Great! Well done.

Now, let's start to pull it all together and to get into action.

> *"Do not worry if you have built your castles in the air. They are where they should be. Now put the foundations under them."*
>
> **Henry David Thoreau**

Making It Real

Let's make all this dreaming real!

ACTION

Please look back over:

1. Your answers to the Three Questions
2. Your answers to This One Goes to 11!

Now you are going to create some exciting, and specific goals for yourself.

For each area of your life from the previous exercise, choose something you would like to make real in your life. It can be something you'd like to realize by next week, or within twenty-five years—any time period is fine.

For example, you might say that in the area of work, you'd like to be self-employed as a fashion designer within three years. In the area of health, you might want to run a triathlon within one year. In the area of community, you might want to be an active contributor to your town's landscaping beauty, and want this over your whole lifetime.

Let all the answers from the exercises you've just done inform and inspire you. Get specific and get excited.

You *are* going to do these things. This is where the rubber meets the road. The point of looking more deeply into what you want is to then take that and make it real. So—get on it, have fun, be brave, maybe a little outrageous, and put down some goals for your life. Go for it!

Remember the dying guy from the video—he didn't get the privilege of completing this sheet. His time was up. And also remember—you're dying too! We all are! You've got a tool in your hands that can make an enormous difference to the richness of your life. Use it!

Well done. Feeling inspired? And perhaps a little scared? What!… not scared? That means you didn't stretch. Go back and put in a few goals that scare you a little. You'll love it! That's where your aliveness is! That's how you create Woohoo!

Get SMART

Ok. So now that you are looking at a sheet with specific goals, let's take the next steps. Make sure they are SMART. Sure, you know this, but make sure you do it.

This is my version of SMART…

1. **Specific**: The more precise and clear you can make your goals, the better. "Take a vacation in spring" isn't as powerful as "Take ten days in Jamaica in May to study Nyabinghi drumming with Rastafarian elders." (What?)

2. **Measurable**: How will you know if you have accomplished it? "Lose weight" vs. "Weigh 185 lbs" or "Weigh 130 lbs." Get it? Have a concrete finish line.

3. **Awesome**: Go for it! Go big, or go home. You are designing your *life* here. Dream big. Here's why. You are designing the "game" of your life, and this game is what's going to turn you into the person you are capable of becoming. Don't wimp out. We've got enough wimps walking the globe. Be bigger than that. Be bigger than your fear. It's just fear.

   You'll see something magical happen. When you go big, you unleash massive energy to get you there. Your character will respond in proportion to that which you ask of it. Ask big, and ye shall receive big. And ultimately, you are actually saying you want to *give* big—to give your biggest and best to the world. Don't be stingy—let yourself rip. That's what we all want from you more than anything else. That's the number one thing. You'll inspire us and give us permission to do the same. Make your goals awesome.

4. **Resonant**: Make sure your goals are resonant—that they thrill you, and fill you with energy and aliveness. If they don't, they are likely too small or driven by your ego. You should get a warm fuzzy feeling thinking about your goals, and probably a little tingly fear too.

5. **Timed**: Give yourself a deadline and make yourself accountable to someone. There is nothing like a little fire under the feet to help get the energy and courage to get things done.

Make it Happen

You've made sure your goals are SMART. Feel the energy and possibility in each goal. Feel how important this is to your living well.

Now, let's make it happen. Here's how:

ACTION

For each goal on your Goals for Life sheet:

See that end result and ask yourself: to have that accomplished by then, what needs to have happened along the way? Reverse engineer it! See the final product and determine what will need to have happened, and how you will need to have made that happen. In other words, lay out (in reverse) the game plan.

For (a silly) example, to be able to bake pies with peaches from my own garden, I'll need a mature peach tree and a recipe. How do I end up with that? I need a peach tree big enough to produce peaches. How long does that take? What does a tree need to thrive, where will I plant it and by when, where will I buy it, etc. I'll need a recipe—where can I get a great one? etc.

Or, to weigh 185 lbs in four months, I'll need to…

Or, to have a book published by next October 1, I'll need to have done the following…

When you work back from the goal through what steps you'll need to take along the way, you end up back here at the present. This all leads to your step number one. Figure out what the *first step* you can take for each goal is. It may be a tiny one such as "Go online to research potential house trades in Europe," or it may be a more daunting one such as "call Dad and tell him I forgive him for missing my wedding."

Whatever it is, for each of your goals, work back to have a game plan for accomplishing each one. Boil it all down to a first step you can commit to taking now.

Collect a handful of first steps, schedule them on the calendar, and get on it! Go. Get in the game! Get excited to create the life you want. This is *exactly* how it's done. It's no big secret. See what you want, make a game plan, and execute it.

ACTION

For each goal, you've answered what steps you will need to take. Now, also ask these powerful questions:

1. Who will I need to *be* to take those steps and make this happen? Get clear, and *be* that person.
2. What will I have to say *yes* to?
3. What will I have to say *no* to?
4. What might get in my way, and how will I deal with that?

Clearly, you're going to need to be a bigger person than you've been in the habit of being, and you're going to have to develop new habits. Habits are essentially what you say *yes* to, and *no* to. Decide what you'll commit to doing and not doing to accomplish your goals.

You might need to say *yes* to waking up thirty minutes earlier to meditate, to eating oatmeal instead of croissants, to reading inspiring writers during lunch, to playing with your son when he asks you to, or to being brave. You might need to say *no* to several hours of television, to hanging out with "energy vampires" (e.g., negative people), to pleasing your boss over your family, or to going to bed too late. You get the picture.

In any case, you can be sure that you are going to need to say *yes* to "stretching out of your comfort zone." That's where you will be growing and coming alive—outside of your current comfort zone. And get excited—sure, it's scary, but it's so damned rewarding!

Making Woohoo! Happen

In later chapters of this book, we'll cover the strategy for building the financial wealth you want. But that still leaves us with the question, "How do I create the Woohoo! I want?"

That's exactly what we've been working on so far:

1. You've committed to doing a better job of listening to what your heart, spirit, and soul want.

2. You've answered the Three Questions to connect more deeply with what matters most to you in life.

3. In This One Goes to 11, you've gotten more specific and vivid in the vision of the life you want. You've clarified what you must have, do and be to thrive.

4. In Making it Real, you've taken all that vision and desire and translated it into very specific goals. You are declaring, "This is what I intend to create in my life to thrive! I believe that accomplishing these specific goals by these specific times is my path to creating energy, purpose, success and meaning in my life. By committing myself to these goals, I am saying to the world: 'This is who I am, this is what I want, and this is what I'm here to give!'"

Are you getting this top-down approach to connecting with who you are, what matters, what you want, and what you are specifically going for? Isn't it both logical and beautiful?

> *"It is out there, outside the confines of our comforts and the pleasure of our accumulations, beyond our architecture of the routine, that we slip the bonds of our limiting beliefs, soar magnificently above our own shortcomings, and express our highest selves."*
>
> **Brendon Burchard**

Having Trouble? Get Help!

If you haven't found new clarity, I have a suggestion. Hire a coach to take you through this. Contact me for one-on-one coaching, or find a Kinder Institute Registered Life Planner (at **www.kinderinstitute.com/dir**), or contact the Coaches Training Institute (CTI) (at **www.thecoaches.com**) for a referral to a life coach (all of whom are trained to help you clarify what you want in life).

Some people will totally connect with want they want from doing the exercises in this book. Others will want to have a coach guide and inspire them.

One of the challenges of doing this alone in your head is that you can bump into the same walls you always bump into. You might not really give yourself permission to dream the way a coach can inspire you to dream.

So just check in with yourself—if you feel a new sense of clarity and energy about what you want from doing these exercises, wonderful! Carry on.

If you don't, then don't give up. Pillar #6 is about getting help. Do that now! The rest of this book is built around the assumption that you have additional clarity about what you want, so dive in to get that. There are countless books and programs designed to help clarify that. The point is, DO something about it. And my opinion is that the most powerful thing you can do is hire a coach, a mentor or a guide of some sort. Their job is to hold you higher than you hold yourself, to see more possibility for you than you see for yourself, and to inspire you to feel the permission and courage to really dream about what you want in and from life. And then to hold your dream for you, and to be a champion of it and of you. To encourage and inspire you onward towards it.

Now, as with anything in life, it's just empty promises until you actually take action. And you know what really inspires action? Support, community and accountability—not in the "report to the domineering boss" kind of way, but in having someone help you account for where you stand and the progress you are making. Get help. Pick your spouse or your best friend, or call me. Get a coach. Get someone on your team who can (1) understand that this means a LOT to you, and that you intend to make these goals real, and (2) be a source of support and accountability for you. There are people who will be thrilled to help lift you to the heights you'll achieve. Use them! It's part of the gift *they* have to give to the world—allow them that privilege.

Keep in mind that spouses, family, or best friends can feel threatened by seeing you commit to creating the life you want. They may fear being left behind by you, or losing the ability to "manipulate" you. Conversely, they might not feel threatened, but may go too easy on you, not really holding you accountable. Be aware of this as you choose your support community.

CHAPTER 7

Pillar #3: Know Your Obstacles

If it were easy to become wealthy, a lot more people would accomplish it. Obviously, there are some obstacles in the way, right?

What are the odds you'll thrive personally and financially without identifying some of the major factors standing in your way? Without becoming aware of what's likely to derail you?

Surely, the odds are a lot higher when you get clear about what holds *all of us* back in general and what holds *you* back in particular.

Some people at this point think, "Ah, c'mon. Just get to the part where we talk about how to make money." That's natural—and that's a problem.

If you never stop to consider what the obstacles are, they keep blocking you.

We've got to become *aware* of them and overcome them.

When it comes to building Woohoo! Wealth, there are basically three areas where you will encounter obstacles:

1. Wiring: In your physical brain wiring.
2. Programming: In your emotions and belief systems.
3. Behavior: In the actions and habits that result from your wiring and programming.

Ready for some bad news?
1. We aren't wired for wealth.
2. We aren't programmed for wealth.
3. We don't practice the habits of wealth.

Bummer! Might as well pack it in and pick up a different book.
Nah—don't worry. We can do this.

If I were to really dive deep into each of these issues, this book would be 500 pages long. My goal here isn't to offer a comprehensive course on the obstacles to wealth. There are fantastic books on that topic already. My goal is to awaken you to these obstacles, get you intrigued by them, and inspire you to take control of them by learning more.

Faulty Wiring (or, Your Brain Sucks at Money)

Modern neuroscience, neuroeconomics, behavioral finance, and cognitive psychology are breaking amazing ground in teaching us about money and our brains. One of the most powerful things you can do to become wealthy is to become more aware of how your brain works, and when it's most likely to block your way to wealth. Our brains are terribly flawed at handling money and economic decisions.

Modern Times

You've seen movies where the characters time-travel to the future and have their minds blown by that advanced world? Well, when it comes to money, that's pretty much how our brains feel.

The cultural evolution of our society has changed at light speed compared to the biological evolution of our brain wiring. We come into this world hardwired for a world that no longer exists. That's just how evolution works.

For example, for most of existence, it made a lot of sense for man to consume food as completely and quickly as he could. The next source of nourishment was typically unknown or uncertain. Our bodies are designed to store excess caloric intake as fat for later sustenance and survival. The concept of saving some food for later isn't well wired into our system.

When you think about it, money is an extremely new invention for mankind. Our hardware is not designed to deal with money, accumulating, or assigning value to things that grow over time. We've always been wired to consume immediately, and we still are. We even consume what we don't have (on credit). Did you realize that humans are the only animals on the planet able to delay gratification for more than a few minutes?

The ability to accumulate assets in one place is only an invention of the last several thousand years. The *need* to accumulate might also be. Did you know that Neolithic man had an average life expectancy of twenty years? Even in the medieval era, thirty years was average. For most of evolution, we have had neither money nor a long life for which we needed to save money! Our hunting and gathering roots lay more in consuming than in planning and accumulating.

A Peek Into Our Brain

Neuroscience and neuroeconomics (the study of decision-making) is increasingly able to point to where in the brain our money behaviors come from.

For example, research indicates that an area of the brain called the amygdala is directly connected to our fear of losing money. (For example, research subjects with damaged amygdalae place fearless (i.e., stupid) economic gambles. They demonstrate no aversion to economic loss.)

Researchers are able to monitor brain activity during various financial or economic decision-making processes, and can see that the limbic system (the mid-level or "mammalian" brain connected to reward) is most active during impulsive decisions for immediate reward. The more modern, logical brain, the neocortex, is more active when weighing the value of future benefits.

The more researchers discover, the more they can see how our brain works with money, and the more flaws they find in how the brain works around money. We believe ourselves to be quite smart and rational beings (and modern economics is based on that supposition), but research tears that misconception to shreds.

Your Brain on Money

Here's a quick fly through some of the major findings of Behavioral Finance to give you a sampling of ways our brain fails us (a veritable pupu platter of faulty functioning):

Our brain manages the massive complexity of our world by building "rules of thumb" called heuristics. And then we live by these rules of thumb. That's a great way to simplify life, except when the rules of thumb are mostly broken. Here are some examples of the flaws we live by:

- We *anchor*—when we pay $28,000 for a car that had a sticker price of $30,000, we're happy. We feel we got a good deal, because we "anchored" on $30K being its value. But the dealership only put that sticker price there to make you think you got good value. The car's actually worth $28K (until you drive it off the lot, that is).

  Infomercials sell to us by slashing prices in half, then doubling the number of knives they include, knowing you've anchored on the first price and number of knives included. ("You mean instead of ten knives for $40, I get twenty knives for $20? What a deal!") Tricky, tricky.

- We have *confirmation bias* (selective hearing; seeking information which supports our view) and rationalize away or ignore evidence that disproves our viewpoint.

- *Availability Bias*—we give more credence to more recent information or more vivid stories. We overweight anecdotal evidence relative to statistically sound evidence (e.g., more people buy lottery tickets right after someone has won a huge sum).

- *Hindsight bias*—an outcome always seems more obvious after the fact. Everybody seems to have seen the big financial crisis coming *after* it came.

- *Mental accounting*—we separate money into different mental accounts and treat it differently, even though it's all the same money. Our tax refund tends to be "free money—Yay!"

- **Prospect Theory** illustrates that we fear loss more than we enjoy gain. Losing $20 hurts more than winning $20 pleases. Twice as much. We aren't rational—we are loss averse.

- **The Disposition Effect** has us wanting good feelings now and delaying pain until later. This typically leads us to hold losing stocks (we wait to feel the pain of "admitting" the loss) and sell winners now ("Yay—I'm up! Sell!"). Not usually a great investment strategy.

- We are **overconfident**—we tend to believe that trends will continue ("I'm on a roll!") or must change ("after five blacks, the next Roulette spin will *surely* come up red!").

- We follow the **herd**—we suffer from "Groupthink." We prefer to do what we see others doing (even if it means staying in a burning building! Really!).

In addition to this sampling of the lessons from Behavioral Finance, Neuroeconomics offers us these nuggets:

- Our "midbrain" is our wanting system and seeks to acquire resources to ensure our survival. This requires that we take risk and expend effort. To induce us to do so, this wanting brain makes acquiring resources (e.g., food, sex) very pleasurable. Makes sense. The problem: We can get this area too primed and too activated relative to our "smarter, more logical" prefrontal cortex. This can lead us to take on excessive risk in the hunger for pleasure (e.g., acquiring money).

  Want evidence? Researchers have found that men shown pornographic pictures (thus activating the pleasure part of the brain) will allocate portfolios more towards risk than men who have not seen those photos. That part of the brain gets lit up and then impacts their economic decision-making.

- Our brain processes economic decisions using three parts of the brain: the ancient midbrain "wants," the temporal lobe "worries" (assesses risk), and the newest prefrontal cortex "calculates" what to do. We *feel* economic risk the same way we *feel* roller-coaster fear. It's physiological. Yet we can reduce our fear response through familiarity. What's the issue? You can be too risk averse when your body *feels* an unfamiliar risk (e.g., newbie investors selling at the slightest market volatility) or too risk-tolerant when you are used to big gambles (e.g., rogue trader loses $1 billion for their firm. Duh!).

- *New* information stimulates the reward part of the brain. Thus we constantly seek it out. We overvalue it. We have a hard time discriminating "signal" (important information) from "noise" (insignificant information) in all the economic data that comes our way. We trade on meaningless "news" rather than on solid "fundamentals" (relevant data).

- Our brains manage the flow of massive amounts of information by making subconscious "good enough" decisions on autopilot. The strongest neural pathways are most likely to get used, even when faced with information that would suggest another route is better. We're on autopilot way more than we realize, and this leads to sub-optimal irrational decisions, because our brain doesn't have the capacity to constantly be optimal.

OK. I think you are getting the point. We're not nearly as rational, in control, or smart as we think we are around money and wealth. We just aren't *wired* to be. And, for the most part, we are unaware of these biases and mental shortcuts.

Here's another way our brains make it hard for us to become wealthy:

The Curse of Habituation

You turn on your air conditioner, and your room suddenly has that new whirring noise in it. Five minutes later, you don't even notice it unless someone points it out. Similarly, you might stop hearing a leaking faucet, or a distant car alarm, or you might have a tag that scratches you a bit, which you eventually stop noticing.

All of these are examples of "habituation," which is a fancy psychological term for "getting used to it." You can also think of it as "normalizing." Something unusual eventually becomes normal. When we have a repeated and constant stimulus, our brains quickly put that in the background of our attention. This is most helpful for keeping our bandwidth open for important stuff such as actual threats (tiger!) or great opportunities (food!).

Why am I introducing this concept? Because while it's a godsend, it's also a curse. I'll explain. We've already set the context that our modern culture conditions us to believe (or act as though we believe) that "I'll be happy when…" I get the new car, I go to the Bahamas, I cut my hair, I get that boyfriend, I get that job, I live in that house, etc. And in the absence of being really clear about what we most deeply want and what *does* bring us deep fulfillment, we play this game of pursuing the good feeling we get from getting what we *believe* will make us happy.

Research in the field of positive psychology illustrates that our pleasure tends to be highest when we are *in anticipation* of getting the thing we want, just *after* we see or decide we are going to get it, and just *before* it is ours. That's our peak. It's downhill from there. We experience the joy of having it (which a Buddhist might claim is the temporary relief from wanting). And then... habituation.

In plain English: you get used to it. It becomes normal. It's decreasingly special. And it's power to engender happiness in you decreases over time, sometimes amazingly rapidly.

It's just the way we're made. Positive Psychology also calls it the Hedonic Treadmill, which suggests that we have a tendency to quickly resume our stable level of happiness after positive or negative events. We're stuck in an endless pursuit of advancement towards happiness that never actually really gets us there, because our happiness keeps getting reset to its default.

Here are a few examples from my life.

Several years ago, I finally bought my dream car—the Acura NSX (it's like a Japanese Ferrari). It was such a thrill to consider that I was actually going to get it, to shop around, and then to finally have it; to hear the engine growl, to shift from third to fourth (where it really comes alive) and to take it to the racetrack and let 'er rip! It was pretty great.

And really, the joy dropped off pretty quickly. A few months in, I felt kind of embarrassed to be driving a flashy car; it took too much attention to keep it clean and free of dents, service was expensive, and I was used to it—it no longer held the same thrill it had. It became normal. Having believed that the NSX would contribute to my well-being, I now saw that I was exactly the same guy with a few more thrills under my belt, but nothing of real importance. I quickly adjusted to this new reality, and it ceased to be special. So I sold it.

Another example: The Police was my favorite band in high school. Being a drummer, I worshipped their drummer, Stewart Copeland. When the long-defunct band announced a reunion and tour, I was thrilled. I did something I'd never done—I entered Ticketmaster's online bidding for front row seats… and got them. Boom! Front row center for The Police. Yeehaa!

Cut to the concert: the anticipation is crazy; the crowd is going wild. The Police come on stage, and there they are; jamming just yards away from me! It was so exciting. I was in heaven. Then they played another song, then another… then another. By about ten songs in, I have to admit that my thrill level wasn't that much higher than if I had been in the nosebleed seats. In fact, my sister and her husband had separately gotten tickets pretty far back, and I called them to switch seats to give them the thrill that had worn off for my wife and me.

Or another example: during the eighteen months I took off from work, while traveling with my family, we lived in Provence for two months. I remember well the day when I finally declared: "OK. I can only take so much leisure!" I was living what millions dream about and, while it was still fantastic, it had become normal, and I was satiated. My spirit was craving to be creative, constructive, and purposeful more than it was craving a break. If you were to drop me from a rough week any other time to that same place, it would be fresh and exciting again. But habituation usually robs us of enduring pleasure from things and experiences.

This needn't always be the case. Gratitude is a powerful antidote. So is buying the *right* things and experiences. And so is buying experiences over things. Recent research is substantiating that you derive more pleasure from spending on others than you do from spending on yourself!

As people climb the socioeconomic ladder, increasing their income or net worth, the anticipated happiness that was supposed to come with it is typically fleeting (and lower than expected). Look to your own life—you've probably had times when you had fewer financial means than you do now. When you look back, were you really less happy? Has your well-being tracked your financial progress? Probably not. And that's probably because of normalization or habituation. You get used to your bigger apartment, nicer clothes, better vacations, and those aren't that much more special to you now than your previous smaller home, less expensive clothes and more modest vacations were.

A revelation that goes counter to our culture is this: the guy with ten times your wealth feels pretty much the same way about his wealth as you feel about yours. You've both gotten used to it. It's now "normal" for you, and any guy with double your wealth is "rich."

You may have heard of a pretty astounding study done on wealth. Researchers have found that no matter what their current level of net worth, most people say they aren't "rich." When asked what "rich" is, the answer is almost precisely double their current net worth or income. The couple with $25 million says that those with $50 million are "rich." The guy who earns $250,000 a year thinks that $500,000 a year would qualify him as "rich."

Another experience from my years of financial planning that has been illuminating is this: at some point during financial data gathering, my clients and I discuss how much money they spend annually. Almost without exception, people will say "… I mean, our spending is nothing extravagant." And this comes from those spending $50,000 a year and those spending $1 million a year. What *is* extravagant? We'll always be "normal." And there will always be the "more fortunate" who are the real "rich and extravagant."

Are you rich? Is your spending extravagant?

Our brains stand in the way of our wealth by depriving us of the happiness we believed would come from buying or doing certain things.

ACTION

Knowing this, how can your wealth plan consciously avoid this pitfall? What's in your life, your closet, your garage, that you believed would make you happy, but which is now simply a mental burden and a storage cost? What experiences did you buy that somehow don't have any lasting impact on you? What experiences did you buy that still do benefit your life? What activities never get old, and never stop bringing you meaning and pleasure? The goal: start to get clear about where money IS getting you the feelings you sought from it, and where it's not. When you spend money, ask yourself: how did it make me feel, how did I like that, and how long did it last? This will help to make you a wise spender.

Terrible Predictors

In his fantastic book, *Stumbling on Happiness*, Daniel Gilbert illustrates that our brains are actually terrible mechanisms for predicting our future happiness. They are usually way off when estimating how much something will contribute to our well-being. Rather, he suggests, a more reliable method is to ask those in the circumstance you want to be in (who bought that thing or have that job or took that trip or live in that neighborhood) how happy they are. Sample *that* population on the measure important to you. You are more likely to find the reality of what it's like than your brain is to predict it correctly.

You want to know a great place to apply that? Having lots of money. Your brain does a poor job of estimating how happy it will make you. We live in a culture that covets wealth and has forever programmed us to believe that once we get there, life will be great.

These have been some examples of how your brain *wiring*—the way your brain works—serves as an obstacle to good decision-making in building wealth. This explains a great deal about why more people aren't wealthy.

Now, let's look at another powerful obstacle. Again, this will be a quick tour, with the hope that you'll be prompted to learn more and take control of this obstacle.

Your Money Programming

While the last section was about our hardware, this one is about our software. At the risk of being unromantic and overly technical, we are essentially animal computers with hardware (a brain) that carries software programming (beliefs). Much the way a computer is unaware of its programming, we are, for the most part, unconscious of our own.

Most of the self-help and personal growth industry revolves around helping people see (1) *that* they are programmed, (2) *what* their programming is and (3) *how* to take control of it and reprogram it to better serve them.

What's programming? Essentially, it's your belief system. A whole bunch of beliefs about who you are, what the world is, how it works, what to do under different circumstances, etc. We have maps, models, and schematics about the way things are and the way things work. It's our *story* about who we are and how the world is. We're typically unaware of it because "that's just the way things *are*." They are so true (to us) that we don't even consider them a personal belief—they are a statement of fact about the way *IT is*!

And our thoughts lead to our feelings. And our feelings lead to our actions. Thus our thoughts lead to our actions. The thoughts you hold directly impact the actions you take. And building wealth takes action. Thus the thoughts you hold will greatly impact your ability to build wealth. Make sense?

You Are Programmed

"It is the mark of an educated mind to be able to entertain a thought without accepting it."

Aristotle

As you sit reading this, you are absolutely and totally programmed about wealth. No question about it. You hold an extremely complex and powerful system of beliefs about wealth, money, people who have money and people who don't, how easy or hard it is to get money, how much you need to be happy, and how good or evil it is. For your entire life, almost without any conscious awareness of it, your computer has had its software coded into it, line by line, and it's fully functioning in you, right now. Please take that as an unquestionable truth (look at me trying to program your software!).

You have a relationship with money. That's another way of saying you have a system of beliefs about money, wealth, getting rich, being poor, that is the sum total of all your life learning, experiences and decisions. We all do.

Here's a quick illustration. Imagine yourself getting out of a dugout canoe and wandering into a tiny and completely remote tribal village deep in a "developing world" jungle. A beautifully adorned barefoot man in a loincloth approaches you and looks you kindly in the eye. Suddenly, from the heavens comes a voice that asks you both the following questions:

"What do you believe about money?"
"How does one become wealthy?"
"If I gave you $100, what would you do with it?"
"What do you think of people who have $100 million?"

As these questions are asked, each of you answers. It's not hard to imagine that your answers are going to be vastly different from the local's answer. Why? Because each of you has different beliefs, experiences, and knowledge about money and wealth. For all we know, the guy might ask, "What's money?"

The world is full of *universal* truths (e.g., "Gravity pulls objects down," or "Humans long to love"). Our belief systems may have some overlap with universal truths, but for the most part, they are just our *personal* truths.

A hugely powerful step in building wealth is learning to differentiate between the two, becoming aware of what *personal* truths (e.g., rich people are greedy) you are holding to be *universal* truths, and then getting more intentional about what you choose to believe.

Fortunately, we are free to believe whatever we want to believe. There are scientific truths that we'd do well to respect, and there are beliefs about the way the world is or the way we are. We are free to construct those as we choose.

In that freedom to believe what we want to believe, we can choose to believe what will fuel our success and Woohoo! Wealth.

To quickly illustrate, let's take the statement "I'm terrible at money." Millions of people hold this to be a truth (as in there's no arguing it, it just *is*). Clearly, this truth, or programming, doesn't sound particularly helpful for building wealth. "I'm on a thrilling adventure to master money" could describe the exact same circumstances, and it's easy to see how much more this would fuel success. The first is hopeless and rigid, whereas the second has hope, flexibility and direction. Neither is more true than the other, yet they lead to very different feelings and thus different actions.

We all have money programming. Wealth programming. Success programming. Yes—YOU do!

"We don't see things the way they are. We see them the way WE are."

Talmud

You're aren't likely to become wealthy until you become aware of your programming, tear it out, and reprogram it for wealth and Woohoo! Creating wealth requires that we overcome our limiting beliefs—that we create a *mindset* or programming that fuels us and serves us.

T. Harv Eker, author of *The Secrets of the Millionaire Mind,* uses the analogy of the thermostat. We all have a wealth "thermostat" setting. We are programmed for a certain level of wealth and success. A thermostat kicks up the heat when it gets cold and cranks the air conditioning when it gets hot—thus ensuring that the room stays at the temperature set on the thermostat.

Likewise, we have a mechanism that kicks in to juice up our wealth when it falls below our "set point," and to actually sabotage (drain) our wealth when we get too far above our programmed set point. I can't back that up with science, but it's a helpful metaphor.

You want to know what wealth level your thermostat is set for?

Look around.

That.

Exactly the life and the wealth you have now. Really? Yup. If we put Donald Trump into your shoes, how long do you think his wealth would remain at your level? Not long—his thermostat is set for billions. If we took a so-called "bum" and put him into exactly your life circumstance, how long would he hold onto the money? Not long. His thermostat is pretty much set for a few bucks.

We all live life with a construct of who we are. And research shows that we then seek evidence to support that construct, while overlooking evidence to the contrary. It's called *self-image*, and it's extremely powerful. Our psyche hates being confronted with evidence that breaks our self-image and wants very much to remain in its comfort zone. (Sounds like our old friend the "ego," doesn't it?)

Here's one way to see it: when you are far from home and nobody knows you, why do you still act like yourself? Technically, you are free to be absolutely anybody you want to be, right? If you tend to be serious and analytical at home, you could be a total silly goofball elsewhere. Nobody would say, "Hey—wait a second; that's not *you!*" No. Your self-image guides you and tells you who to be, because that's who you *believe* yourself to be.

Until you become aware of what part of your self-image stands at odds with what and *who* you need to be to be wealthy, it'll be hard to achieve wealth.

> *"Man alone, of all creatures of earth, can change his thought pattern and become the architect of his destiny."*
> **Spencer W. Kimball**

One of the most common tugs-of-war in our culture is this one: On the one hand, we believe, "I want to be rich," and on the other hand, we believe, "rich people are greedy evil pigs." As long as you hold onto that latter belief, how will your self-image of being a great person ever allow you to join the ranks of the greedy evil pigs? It won't. You'll sabotage your wealth-building efforts as long as you hold as "self-evident truths" any beliefs that don't jive with your self-image.

> **You've got to get clear on who you believe yourself to be and what you believe about wealth, and then get clear about which of those beliefs is an anchor holding you back from becoming the wealthy person you want to be. And then you must choose to adopt belief systems that will perpetuate wealth-building behavior. You replace your *default* programming with your *conscious* programming.**

We live into our stories. One of the most powerful ways to become wealthy is to write that story (that you are a person of increasing wealth) and believe it—live into it.

You will always act in accordance with what you most believe, and those actions will create your results.

Here's an example. One of the most anti-wealth programs we can hold is the victim mindset. We believe that our wealth circumstances are the result of a huge variety of outside forces beyond our control. We are the victims of circumstances. We blame others, events, and bad luck for our not being wealthy, and we do it so long and believe it so much that we can eventually come to give up, helpless in our quest for what we want. Wouldn't you want to tear out this programming and replace it with something like: "I take 100% responsibility for all of the results I have in my life; I have the ability to create wealth, and I'm doing it!"?

How and where did we get this programming?

Life. Being human. Evolution. It's just the way it works.

First and foremost, we got our beliefs from others. We are programmed to imitate other people (again—researchers have shown we'll stay in a burning building if we see others doing the same). We get our beliefs from our culture, our times, our neighbors, our families, our friends, our schools, and our media. All you have to do is see how differently programmed the various peoples of the earth are to recognize that we all construct different views of reality. These are not truth. Rather, they are perspectives or paradigms.

Where do we get our money beliefs? Our money messages? Our "money scripts" (i.e., the stories that keep getting played over and over again in our heads and drive our behavior)? Let's understand that.

Our money beliefs come mainly from three places:

1. What we were taught.

2. What we were shown.

3. What we experienced.

What we were taught

All of our lives, people have told us what they believe to be true about money. During our most formative years, our parents, family, friends, TV and radio spoke directly at us and said, "*This* is true about money."

"Money doesn't grow on trees."

"Go ask your father; he has all the money."

"Money is the root of all evil."

"Sure, go ahead and buy it; we can afford it."

"Having money isn't for people like us."

"You've got to work really hard for money."

"If only we had more money, life would be fine."

"It takes money to make money."

Our sweet little innocent brains responded with, "Got it. Understood. That's true about money. If mommy said so, then it is."

Day after day, year after year, the "lines of coding" got programmed into our minds. Our worldview about money emerged. And we believed it. And for the most part, we still do.

Here's an example from my life: I grew up very fortunate and with parents who never said, "we can't afford it." Sure, they said *no* all the time and had healthy limits, yet our family could do what we wanted, have what we wanted, and give what we wanted. Guess what my challenge as an adult is? The belief that "there's always money, and we can always afford it."

Another example: In his book, *Down the Garden Path*, Beverly Nichols reflects on the poverty of his youth and recounts the story of asking his mother why they don't have a greenhouse to grow grapes. She replies, "[how] terribly expensive it is to own a greenhouse." As an adult, Nichols recognizes that "the childish impressions of economics are never obliterated." He marvels at how, as an adult who now owns a greenhouse that is actually of very little cost, he "trembles to think of the extravagance of it all. 'This is folly…this is reckless squandering…'" his subconscious mind tells him, even though his conscious mind reassures him, all because his mother once told him that hot-houses were terribly expensive.

ACTION

Want to find out what you might have been taught about money? Do this exercise:

Think back to when you were a child. Try to remember what you were taught about money, wealth, wealthy people and success. Think of your earliest money memories. Write it all down. Start to bring awareness to what messages were given to you by family, friends, society, or media.

ACTION, continued

Now look back over those. Circle the handful that feel most emotionally "charged" or strong to you.

And now, look to your current life. In what ways are you holding those beliefs? Are the things you were taught about money as a child the things you believe to be true about money today? Find the connection. When you do, you'll be pulling back the proverbial curtain to see the wizard who is controlling your money beliefs.

What we were shown

What people say and do are often very different things. In addition to being taught "truths" about money throughout life, we learned what we learned about money by *observing* people in *action* with money. Put differently, we had truths about money modeled for us. We watched our parents, siblings and friends dealing with money, and we took it all in.

If Dad spent a lot on clothes, we learned that's what you do with money. If we watched Mom clip coupons, we learned that's what we do with money. If we heard them complain about bills and turn away requests for charity, that left a mark. If we saw Dad working hard to afford private school tuition, we learned lessons from that.

That is, in addition to what we were *told* about money, we *witnessed* the reality of money passing through our lives, and it shaped our belief system about money. It shaped yours.

I grew up watching my dad typically get the higher-quality items at a store and then get some extra things just in case. When we went shopping before going off to camp, he selected all sorts of great equipment for us, and picked up a couple extra items we "might need." Guess who does the same today?

What are some of your memories about how your parents dealt with money growing up? What were their habits and their emotions around money? Was it a joyous thing? A stressful thing? Was there abundance or scarcity? Arguments? Avoidance?

Write down everything you can think of that you learned from watching your parents, family and friends when you were growing up.

Great. Now. How is that alive in you today? Are you repeating the money relationship your parents had? Are you rebelling and doing the exact opposite (as in "I'll *never* forego ice cream when *I'm* grown up!" or "I'll never fly First Class with the snobs when I grow up"?)

What we experienced

In addition to what we were taught and what we had modeled for us, we had our own experiences with money, some of them extremely formative. When emotionally charged experiences involve money, we tend to have those seared into our brains.

I remember getting ready to go to the mountains for four days with my best friend and his family, when I was about 10. As I was going, my dad asked if I had any money. I didn't, and hadn't even considered how money might come into the equation. He reached into his wallet and gave me $60. Three crisp twenties. Had I tried to guess what amount he was about to hand me, I would have thought about $4 (enough to cover what I thought was important—a bit of candy). What he did give me felt like $1,000. Whoa! His estimation of what I might need was totally reasonable from his standpoint. I was *rich* from my standpoint.

The point is, I got a money message that carries strong with me today: I love having money because of all the freedom and possibility it affords me. Having lots of money is a good feeling.

On another occasion—perhaps I was 8 years old—I remember being on a trip with my family and sitting in a restaurant for dinner. I was reading the menu and looking exclusively at the prices on the right, trying to find the least expensive thing available. Somewhere in my head was the awakening realization that I was costing my family money, and I was feeling a burden because of it. When the waitress took my order, I ordered a hot dog. This being unusual for me, my mom asked me what was up. I admitted that I was ordering the least expensive item I could find. With a sweet, warm smile and a poignant sort of "awwww," she reassured me that I was welcome to have anything I wanted on the menu and didn't need to be concerned about the price. My dad's amused and supportive smile confirmed it.

How do you think that played into my money scripts? Do you think I've always been really cautious about prices on menus? Good guess. Not really. "We can afford it."

Interestingly, my two sisters have really different money messages from mine. They are much more frugal.

Julia, a friend of mine, remembers the day her "less fortunate" cousin Nicole came to visit. At the end of a long day, Julia's dad wanted to leave Nicole with a little gift—some pocket money. As he had no money with him, he turned to Julia and asked her for $10. He promised to pay her back. Julia gave him the money and he handed her ten dollars to Nicole, looking very magnanimous, and sent her on her way with a "Here's a little pocket money—get yourself something fun." Her dad never repaid her. How do you think Julia feels about lending people money today? You got it—"You can't trust people" is in her money script.

ACTION

What experiences can you remember around money from your early life that had a real impact on you? It could have been finding money, losing money, stealing money, winning money, getting cheated, cheating someone else, etc.

When that happened to you, what did you decide was "true" about life and money? Write down anything you can think of. How is that playing out in your life today?

It's just part of being human that early in life we have experiences that make a massive impression on us and form an ingrained belief. We subconsciously do that as a way of coping with a major challenge (or of marking a really pleasant one). By writing a rule and believing it, our brain helps alleviate some feeling that has confronted us in life. It creates a behavior designed to protect us from pain.

If you keep bumping into money problems or major life challenges, it's almost certain that you are bumping against an unconscious belief about the way life is.

The Big 10 Money Beliefs

By now, you've written down a whole bunch of beliefs you have about money, and seen where they might have come from. Be clear that these beliefs are absolutely driving your money behavior and impacting your ability to build financial wealth.

As identified by Rick Kahler, Ted Klontz and Brad Klontz, who are leading practitioners in this area, here are the ten most prevalent money myths in our culture:

1. More money will make things better.
2. Money is bad.

3. I don't deserve money.

4. I deserve to spend money.

5. There will never be enough money.

6. There will always be enough money.

7. Money is unimportant.

8. Money will give me meaning.

9. It's not nice to talk about money.

10. If you are good, the universe will supply all your needs.

Breaking Free From Our Beliefs

You are no longer the young person you were when you created these beliefs to protect you. You are now a different person in different circumstances. It's time to let go of some of the beliefs holding you back, and to replace them with the powerful beliefs that will drive your success.

It's safe to assume we have some supportive money beliefs and some unsupportive ones. You just identified some of yours in the last three actions.

If we want to free ourselves from unsupportive beliefs, how do we do that?

First, I want to suggest that you start with compassion for yourself and others. Why *would* you have a healthy relationship with money? Where in the world would you have seen that modeled for you? Where was it taught to you? Who's been helping you along the way? Money is so taboo that we barely discuss it; most people argue over it, avoid it, blame it, stress over it, overzealously crave it and generally model unhelpful behavior around it. There's no great reason why you should already have this all taken care of.

As a matter of fact, in my years of advising people, I have seldom come across anyone who feels they have a "healthy" or comfortable relationship with money. There's always stress, headaches, fear, greed, mis-information, panic, overspending, underspending, etc.

So feel free to give yourself a break, and be kind to yourself if you don't have it all together when it comes to money.

Second, get in the game and take over. It may not have been your fault, but as of this very sentence—this very moment—it's 100% your responsibility. Nobody else's but yours.

How to Work with Your Programming:

1. Get clear that these are personal beliefs rather than universal truths.
2. Know that they got put into your head. It's not your fault, but it is now your job to change them.
3. Decide that you want to take control of what you believe because it's more fun, more empowering and more constructive. Determine that you want to tear out the programming of unhelpful beliefs.
4. Commit to programming in powerful, helpful beliefs.

How do you do that? The Work

Most money scripts can be managed by bringing them to the light of day and consciously working to choose preferable beliefs.

Perhaps the strongest, simplest method I have found for replacing limiting beliefs with more empowering ones is from Byron Katie; what she calls "The Work." As a first step, get her book *Loving What Is* and read it. It's fantastic.

Katie has created a powerful process for examining our beliefs and replacing them with different truths that serve us better. Rather than go into depth here, I urge you to read the book and start practicing the method.

Here's a brief summary of how to do it:

Take a statement you believe to be true. For example, you might take "Rich people are greedy evil pigs." Find a truth you hold about money that you can see won't serve you on your journey to building wealth. Then apply these four questions and the "turnaround." Ask:

1. Is that true?

While our first instinct is to believe our statement (otherwise it wouldn't be called a belief), this question has us reflect upon the truth of it. Where in the universe is it written that your statement is truth? Consider that. *Are* rich people really greedy evil pigs? Really? Is that true?

2. How can you know that's true?

Go deeper. Can you really know that's true everywhere and always? Is that a fact? Or more likely, is it a position you are taking—a perspective? Might I have plenty of evidence that some rich people are not greedy evil pigs?

3. How does it make you *feel* when you think that thought?

Here, you take a look at what happens to your emotions when you hold that thought as true. What does believing that thought do to you? How does it make you feel? Isn't it stressful to want to be rich, yet believe that you will become greedy and evil? Doesn't it feel hopeless?

4. Who would you be without that thought?

If you were incapable of thinking that thought, how would you be? How would you feel? What might be possible from that perspective? If I didn't believe rich = greedy pig, I would feel so much more at peace, and so much more free to build financial success.

5. The Turnaround:

Now think of every statement you can come up with that is the *opposite* of that thought. Write each one down and consider the truth of that statement. Examples would be: Rich people *aren't* greedy evil pigs; rich people are generous, wonderful humans; or even, *I* am a greedy evil pig.

In trying on alternate truths and seeing the possibility in each, we find the freedom to recognize that what was a truth to us before, is now a choice to us. A freedom. We are free to choose what we believe, free to examine and let go of stressful, painful and unhelpful thoughts.

One of my favorite bumper stickers pretty much sums it all up:

Don't believe everything you think!

Another quick way to take control of some beliefs after you've identified them is to write them down, and then rewrite each belief in a more positive, empowering way.

For example: "Earning money is hard and takes effort" can be reframed as "Using my time, energy and gifts to deliver value to the world is an honor, a privilege and fun!"

In our Woohoo! Wealth Weekend live event, we dive into discovering what your money messages are. We work on tearing those puppies out and replacing them with empowering beliefs to fuel your success.

Get clear and realize that you are absolutely, without a doubt, being run by a belief system you hold about money, wealth, wealthy people and success. Your job is to accept that, unearth your programmed beliefs, consider the ways in which they might be furthering or foiling your quest for wealth, and then consciously create new beliefs that will better serve you.

This goes for any beliefs, not just those about money. It absolutely applies to your beliefs about happiness, fulfillment and Woohoo!.

And again, a powerful method for releasing unsupportive beliefs is to attach pain to continuing to hold onto them. As we did in the Action at the end of Chapter 5, envisioning and feeling the impact that continuing to hold onto this belief will have on your life can link enough pain to it to have you want to drop it. Or, you can wear a rubber band on your wrist and give yourself a massive snap with it anytime you state or think that belief.

ACTION

I stated in the first pages of this book that I am wealthy. Think back. How did you react to reading that? What stories did you make up about me? What positive or negative judgments came up? That's a great place to look at what your programming is around being or becoming wealthy. Did you wish me well and congratulations? Did you feel happy for me? Did you vilify me? Did you feel pity for me? Jealousy? Criticism?

I've got money, and I love my life!

What does that statement do for you? Are you happy for me?

There's an old Huna philosophy that states: "Bless that which you want." Simply put, if you want to be wealthy and love your life, "bless" every person exemplifying that whom you can find. Give them a huge "Good for you!" That will make it much better than making them wrong, inferior, unworthy, etc. You won't allow yourself to become that which you demonize.

You Might Be a Little Wacko

The deeper and more emotional a money script is, the harder it can be to identify and reprogram.

When it comes to money, we often see some really challenging emotions: anxiety, shame, denial, or fear. There are a host of money "disorders" which throw us far off the path to wealth: workaholism, overindebtedness, compulsive spending, financial enabling or dependency, to name but a few.

Let's face it—money is the second most secret and "charged" area of our life (after sex). And it's the number one cause of marital conflict. It's our main cultural taboo.

Money is an area where we might be a little crazy. Millions are. There's no shame in it. Again—why *would* we have a healthy relationship with money? It's worth taking a good look at yourself and asking: "Do I have a problem with money?" Or ask your spouse or best friend. If it looks like you might be a little wacko in your money life, get help. Get in the game of taking care of that. There are great books, money psychologists, traditional therapists, etc. ready and happy to help. Until you do, it'll be a heavy load to carry on the road to wealth.

Your Money Personality

We all have a money personality. It's who we've become after being shaped by all these forces, and it's how we are programmed to act around money. Some great writers have put out really fun and helpful books to help you identify what your money personality is.

Olivia Mellan has written *Money Harmony*, in which she identifies five core money personality "archetypes": the Hoarder, the Spender, the Money Monk, the Amasser and the Avoider. You can take her quiz to find out what your money type is here: **www.moneyharmony.com/ MHQuiz**.

Brent Kessel wrote a great book called *It's Not About the Money*, in which he describes his take on a spectrum of money personalities. He has identified the following eight money types (their names give you clues about their qualities): the Guardian, the Pleasure Seeker, the Idealist, the Saver, the Star, the Innocent, the Caretaker and the Empire Builder. He also has a money type quiz you can take at **http://quiz. brentkessel.com/financial_archetype_top.php**.

We are all driven to seek different feelings from our interactions with money and to avoid certain pains around money. And it's different for everyone. Bringing awareness to what your natural tendencies are around money will help you to find the balance you need to be a more effective wealth builder. And it might help you understand why your mate is such a hoarder or such a spender. There's no right or wrong— just more awareness and the quest for better balance.

Get these books and read them. Get to know your money personality, or come to a Woohoo! Wealth Weekend, where we dive into it.

By now, I hope you've seen that one of the greatest obstacles to creating wealth is how your brain works, and how it's programmed. Your job is to be aware of that, become educated about it, take measures to avoid the pitfalls caused by your hardware (e.g., following the investment herd) and software (e.g., believing "money is dirty").

When you are clear about *how* you work as a wealth-building entity, you are much more powerful at doing it.

Dig in. Figure yourself out. Tear down the old you.

You can rebuild yourself. You have the technology. You have the capability to build Woohoo! Wealth. You *will* be that person. Better than before. Better. Stronger. Faster.

And let me ask you this. Did you know any of this before? Of the topics we've covered in this chapter, how aware were you of those things such as brain wiring and money programming? Probably not very. Let's get back to Pillar #1: Get in the Game! These aren't news. Anybody who's really into building wealth eventually comes to learn this stuff. Books are written about it; Google has pages and pages on it; workshops teach it. It's all out there. Get in the game! Learn this stuff, and get curious and engaged—it will make all the difference. Right on!

You and *Your Unique Obstacles*

While we've focused on some of the most powerful obstacles to building wealth, I also want to make sure to point this out:

As beautiful and unique as you are in your gifts, you also have your own unique set of personal obstacles to creating the life and wealth you want. You have "buttons" that your best friend doesn't have, and you have fears that your sister doesn't have. You have unhealed wounds that your boss doesn't have. Your ego is shouting precise instructions for why *you and you alone* should just hold on a second. I'm not sure *what* it's telling you, I'm just positive *that* it's telling you something.

You want to be attuned to what your own personal obstacles are, and get clear about who you need to be and what you need to do not to be thwarted by them.

We all have fears, insecurities, habits and comfort zones that are killing us. How will you uncover what yours are, and implement strategies to deal with them on your quest for Woohoo! Wealth?

Life Obstacles

And finally, I really want to acknowledge this: you have a complex life full of commitments, demands, responsibilities and restrictions of all sorts. If you are like most people, you have work commitments, family commitments, laundry, dishes, cars to get serviced, and a body to keep running. I get it. I know. Life already feels full to the brim and inflexible in lots of areas. If you have young kids as I do, the demands never end. Between earning a living, feeding a family, keeping a house running, and finding some time to stay healthy and connected with friends, where are you supposed to find the time in your life to hold the commitment to creating Woohoo! Wealth?

That's a powerful question, and one I highly recommend you ask yourself, and find an answer to.

In this game of creating Woohoo! Wealth, your unique playing field is set. There's the goal, on the other side of the field full of obstacles and opponents.

I'm not making any claims that it's easy. There's no doubt that creating the life and wealth you want takes work, together with setbacks and failures.

But let's be really clear. Those obstacles never go away. All great games have obstacles and challenges, setbacks and pains. They are part of the game. And they are the number one reason most people never really do what it takes to create Woohoo! Wealth. "I can't!" is such a comforting and powerful belief. Comforting? Yes—when you give yourself the out from even trying, you choose the comfortable devil you know (and it's a pretty good devil, after all).

The reality of it is that our lives are a direct reflection of what we consider absolutely vital. We have no more or less than that which we are totally committed to having.

If I told you that your ten closest friends and family were going to die unless you determined a way to work with the circumstances (i.e., obstacles) of your life and *still* create the wealth and life you want, do you think you might find the resourcefulness to make that happen? You probably could. That's because the urgency would have just been upgraded from "That would be nice" to "Holy shit—I MUST do it!"

Do you think people with far greater obstacles than yours, with far more challenging circumstances and demands, have created wealth and personal thriving? You bet they have.

Let's get crystal clear: you have obstacles and circumstances *challenging* you, not *preventing* you.

Once again—that's good news. That's what makes the game hard and fun.

And that IS the game of life: to overcome your personal obstacles in order to claim the aliveness your spirit craves.

So, while you'll get my full support and understanding in acknowledging that this game is challenging, and your circumstances may not make it easy, you will also get my total belief that YOU...CAN...DO...IT! You CAN create the life you want, and you CAN thrive. If only you will.

Habits!

The only way we accomplish anything is through our actions. Our actions are driven by our thoughts and feelings. As you rebuild yourself and become bigger, better and stronger, you'll take bigger, better and stronger action towards building wealth. You'll build the habits of wealth.

The rest of this book is about the actions you take to build financial wealth. We're going to transition from the *inner* game of wealth to the *outer* game—the strategic and tactical, real-world game of what to do to end up Woohoo! Wealthy! I'm setting my coach hat aside (but nearby!) and putting on my financial planner hat for a while.

And I hope you can see now that starting with the strategy and tactics would be fruitless. Until you have clarity about what wealth means to you, until you know how mind and mindset play into the equation, your tactics are very likely to be for nothing.

You now have powerful strategies for moving yourself *up* on the Woohoo! Wealth graph. Use them.

CHAPTER 8

Pillar #4: Know Your Numbers

Ok. Here we are, at last, in the more tangible land of dollars and sense, strategy and technique.

So far we've clarified what you really want (what wealth is to you), we've identified inner obstacles on the path, and now we're going to get down and dirty into the numbers.

> **Here's the key: Know your net worth, cash flow, how much spending you need to live the life you want, and know how much you need saved up to sustain that lifestyle forever.**

If you just went "yikes," fear not. This won't hurt.

Here's the pitfall: Most people don't know their financial numbers. They are unclear about what wealth they have, how much they want, and thus how much more they need.

If you don't know where you stand, and where you want to go, then how can you make a realistic plan? Most people have a vague sense of their current financial picture and a vague goal of needing a lot more. It's hard and inefficient to plan that way.

Remember our Woohoo! Wealth Graph? Well, here we'll be working on moving you towards the right—more wealth—and getting you from your current position to your ideal financial life.

The Financial Lifecycle

In life, we all go through a financial lifecycle…

- **Dependence**: We start totally dependent. We need our parents to provide everything for us.
- **Contribution**: Eventually, as children, we start to contribute, not for pay, but for being part of a family and to pull our own weight. We make our beds, take out the trash, do the dishes, etc.
- **Receiving**: Then we might be *given* money—allowance, gifts, etc. We now have purchasing power of our own, and we buy toys and candy.
- **Earning**: We start to earn money. Not enough to support ourselves, but we begin to take part in the economy: Earning, spending, and perhaps saving. We are still financially dependent.
- **Self-supporting**: If all goes well, one day we take or create a job that provides enough income to support us. We detach from the family economic unit and create our own sustainable economy.

From here, it can go in all sorts of directions. Ideally, it goes this way:
- **Building Wealth**: As we earn income and spend, we manage to accumulate assets. Those can be cash savings, stock and bond portfolios, real estate, royalties and patents, a business, land—lots of things. It can be anything that has financial value. This pool of

assets is growing, but is not yet substantial enough to allow us the freedom from having to *actively* earn our income.

- **Financial Freedom**: Finally (for the select few), we cross the magical threshold, the finish line, into the promised land and see that our assets are sufficient to provide us with the money we expect to need to support us for the rest of our lives. And we are then financially free. We no longer *have* to work to have the income we want to support our ideal lifestyle. Financial freedom can have different degrees. You can have enough to support your basic lifestyle, all the way up to having enough to support *any* lifestyle.

- **Transfer**: Our wealth may deplete over the rest of our life, or it may still grow. In either case, what's left when we die gets transferred—the final act in the lifecycle of wealth.

ACTION

Where are you in this lifecycle? Identify the stage.

Most people live stuck in the cycle of paycheck-to-paycheck. Wherever you are, the **name of the game is to get to Financial Freedom**, not because it will make you happy, but because it will serve as powerful fuel for your purpose, and because at some point you will likely *need* to stop actively working due to age, injury, fatigue, or whatever.

So, what does financial freedom look like? This is an important question and most people, once again, have only a vague sense of that.

Income Vs. Net Worth

Let's start by making an important distinction. What do you want: income or net worth, both or neither? What's the difference?

Income is money that comes into your life that you can spend to support the lifestyle you most want. Income can be *active* or *passive*.

Active income results from you exchanging your time or energy for money. Examples are working at a job, managing real estate, putting together deals, creating a painting, and running a business. In other words, it takes a significant amount of your time and/or energy.

Passive income comes to you without requiring significant time or energy on your part. Examples would be stock dividends, bond interest, real estate income that is managed for you, owning a business which doesn't require much of your time, an Internet business that runs by itself, a vending machine, Social Security, pension income, or disability payments.

At some point in your life you are going to want to transition from *earning* income to *receiving* income. In our culture, the two most wanted times for that transition are ASAP or at age 65 (retirement age).

The earlier part of this book addressed our desire for freedom, and that was focused on the freedom to live the life our spirit wants to live. We saw that that has less to do with money and more to do with clarity, intention, strategy and courage.

Here, we are talking about *financial* freedom. That is, **having enough money to support the life we want, with only the amount of *active* paid work we most want**. Now, this is a pretty different definition from what a lot of the finance world will offer. Most will suggest that financial freedom is the freedom to not have to work at all.

Years of seeing people not having to work and not having any driving vision of what they are doing with their lives, has changed my belief that people don't want to work. Rather, people don't want to work at jobs they don't like. People don't want to *have to* work. But people deeply yearn to matter, to contribute, and to be challenged, engaged, and purposeful. Our national image of working hard in order to then retire to the golf course is an empty fantasy for many. I've seen more examples of doctors on the golf course who are miserable for having lost their identity and purpose, than I see thriving golfers.

So, my hurry to help people get work out of the picture has greatly diminished over the years. That said, my dedication to helping them have the *freedom to choose* whether to work has not. And I'm highly dedicated to them having the freedom to choose whether work is *paid* or not.

This reminds me of a client, a teacher, who came to me claiming that she simply *had* to quit her teaching job (the politics were driving her nuts), but she knew she didn't have enough money to do so. Surprisingly, after crunching the numbers, I illustrated that she, in fact, *could* quit! Guess what? Now that work wasn't a *requirement*, but rather a *choice*, she went right back to her job with a new attitude!

Income is the water that comes out of the hose. **Assets** are the reservoir from which it comes.

Income is money that comes into your life.

Assets are a store of value that can be converted into income, or which naturally produces income.

So, which do you want (or which is better)—income or assets?

The better question is, "How can I have sustainable (passive) income for life?"

You can't spend assets. They need to be converted into money to be spent. You can't spend stock or real estate. You can spend the income they generate, or you can sell the asset and receive money that you can spend. (Technically, cash is an asset that can be spent.)

Typically, income already comes in the form of money and can be spent.

What you want is *spendability.*

Thus, you want something that generates income or can be converted into income.

Let's look at two extremes. In this first case, you might be someone who has never saved a dollar in their life, but has spent years working for a large company. You retire with a very generous pension, paying you 150% of the income you need to live, guaranteed for life (with inflation increases). You don't have any assets (as in money in the bank), but you are financially free. It's all income. (And sure, you can consider the pension an asset and even put a value on it, but we're looking more at the *cash flow* nature of it.)

On the other hand, you could have started an Internet company, put every penny into it, then had it go public (become a publicly traded stock) and create $20 million (or $100 billion) for you. Out of work, and with your only asset being a pool of $20 million, you have no income, but you have way more than enough assets to support your desired lifestyle.

Most people end up with a combination: some assets; some income.

The goal is to have the income, whether generated by an income source (e.g., pension) or an asset source (e.g., real estate, stocks, passive business) to support your lifestyle forever.

Think of your wealth as a bucket with water. Your income is a spigot on the bucket. You want to be able to open the spigot to have the flow that quenches your thirst and to feel confident that the bucket is full enough to quench your thirst forever.

For most people, the game plan is to create an asset pool large enough to sustainably produce the needed income. But that won't be for everyone. Plenty of people become financially free from income sources rather than assets. Fire fighters with great pensions are an example of this latter category.

The Two Big Questions

Now that we've covered income versus assets, we see that your financial freedom comes down to these two fundamental questions:

1. How much income do I need to live a thriving life?

2. How much do I need in assets to passively generate that income forever?

Pretty simple, huh? What does it cost to live my desired life, and how much will it take for me to be free to spend that much forever, without *actively* earning it?

Get ready for it…

Pitfall Check

There's about a 90% chance you don't have the answer to that right now. You're looking right at one of the reasons you aren't on the path to Woohoo! Wealth. If you are like most people, you can't tell me your current net worth, your current cash flow, your desired lifestyle spending level, and what asset pool it takes to generate that passively.

It's OK. You are in good company. But let's get real—how are you going to achieve financial freedom, when once again, you haven't defined it (numerically) for yourself? And this one isn't an internal woo woo happy Woohoo! definition. This is just numbers and dollars. The most basic part of achieving any goal is knowing where you stand (point A), what the goal is (point B) and how to get from point A to point B (the plan).

So let's figure it out!!!

Your Numbers

What are some of "your numbers," and why might you want to know them?

Cash Flow: This is simply a statement showing the money that comes into your life (income), the money that goes out of it (expenses), and the difference between the two. If you earn more than you spend, you have positive cash flow. If you spend more than you earn, you are an American... I mean, you have negative cash flow. The difference between what you earn and spend is your savings (positive) or your deficit (negative). If you earn $75K and spend $60K, your net cash flow is a positive $15K.

Net Worth: Your net worth is the difference between everything you own and everything you owe. It's a statement that adds up everything you have of value (assets) on one side, and every debt (liability) you have on the other. And then it subtracts the debt from the assets—the difference is your net worth. (Not as a human being, of course, just your net financial wealth). If you own $500,000 worth of stuff, and you owe $300,000, your Net Worth is $200,000. Simple.

Why might you want to know your Cash Flow and Net Worth?

You want to know your *expenses* so that you know what it costs to live your *current* lifestyle. And that will be the crucial number in defining what it costs to live your *ideal* life (it might be more or less than you are spending now).

You want to know your *income* so that you know if it covers your expenses, and so you can see what's left over to build up savings and thus assets (and net worth).

You want to know your *net worth* so that you know where you currently stand financially. And you want to be able to quantify how much net worth it's going to take to allow you enough passive income to support yourself forever.

With clarity about these numbers, you start to answer these three core questions:

1. What does my ideal life cost?
2. What asset base would allow me to spend that amount sustainably?
3. How much more in assets is it going to take to get from my current spending and net worth to that ideal spending and net worth?

So let's do it! (Note: the next chapter will be about answering the important question: *How* will I build the additional assets I need?)

A lot of people resist numbers, partly because they think they are hard or confusing or boring. I get it. And I also get that if you don't dive into this and figure it out (or get help doing so), you will be on the wandering, drifting, unclear path to wealth and much less likely to achieve financial freedom. So let's do this and get in the game here.

Figuring Out Your Cash Flow

Again, you want to know your cash flow so that (1) you can have an idea of your lifestyle expenses—this will help you figure out your *ideal* expenses—and (2) you'll see how much you are saving (which will play a role in building your assets).

There are a number of ways to figure this out. I'll offer some suggestions here, and you pick what you think works best for you.

1. **Wing it**. If you have a pretty clear idea of what your income is, and you have a pretty clear idea of how much you save (or draw from savings or credit) in a year, then you have enough info for a good start.

    For example, if you have a salary of $100,000, and you know that between your 401(k) and your brokerage account you put away $20,000, then you are spending about $80K (including income taxes).

    Lots of people are in this situation and can pretty quickly back into how much they are earning, spending and saving. Likewise, in the same example, if you earned $100,000 and also needed to draw $20,000 from savings or credit over the year, then you are spending about $120,000 a year.

2. **Add it up.** Another option is to pull out your checkbook (paper or online) and credit card statements, and any accounts that have money coming in and going out, and just start adding up all the income that came in and all the spending that went out. In other words, look at the numbers and build the picture.

    Note that here you don't want to double count the following: if you buy things on your credit card, then pay off the credit card from the checking account, don't double-count both the spending on the card *and* the spending from the checking to pay off the card. Just count the checking spending. In a really simple situation where you have one checking account and everything comes into and out of that account, this method is pretty easy. Just get a year of statements and add up your income, add up your expenses and look at the difference.

3. **Use Quicken, Microsoft Money or Mint.com** to track your expenses. This method takes more work, but provides great results. With Quicken, you set the program up to track your income and expenses, you categorize your income and spending (e.g., restaurants, car service, life insurance) and then get detailed reports illustrating exactly where the money is coming from and going to. Mint.com does this mostly automatically (and free) for you, though you still have to help it. In all cases, you get a really clear picture as long as you keep up with it. I do this, and it only takes me maybe thirty minutes a month to stay on top of it. And I can tell you precisely what my cash flow numbers are.

Or, again, get help. Hire someone to help you figure it out, but pick one of these methods. I'm betting that you'll find it's actually pretty fun, empowering and extremely enlightening to know where your money is going. Do this, and you'll emerge with a sense of what your current lifestyle costs you and also of how much "juice" or savings you have to build your asset base.

Spending Groups:

I split my spending into three groups (each with its own sub-categories):

Mandatory fixed expenses. These are things such as mortgage payments or life insurance premiums. Though nothing is *mandatory* for the life I'm choosing to lead, these are costs that are just a part of it and tend to be the same every month.

Mandatory flexible expenses. These are costs we need to have—food, clothing, entertainment, etc.—that are flexible in terms of how much we spend. We can eat healthy rice and beans, or we can buy prepared meals from fancy stores. In either case, we need food but can really change its cost in our lives.

Discretionary expenses. These are costs that aren't necessary—travel, electronics, spas, etc. that we love to enjoy but can do without.

What makes up these groups will be different for everyone. And they are offered here to help you see that your living expenses have different qualities—some tend to be fixed and required, while others are more flexible. But even the "fixed and required" expenses of mortgage or private tuition are neither. We are free to design completely different lives that fulfill us more.

Build yourself a cash flow statement and get to know how your spending fits into these different categories.

Figuring Out Your Net Worth:

Once you've done that, let's build your net worth statement. This one is pretty easy.

Get out a sheet of paper (or a spreadsheet) and on one side list all of your assets. Include checking accounts, savings accounts, investment accounts, real estate, life insurance cash value, retirement accounts, valuable personal belongings or automobiles, etc., and anything that you own which has value to it. Feel free to ignore furniture and similar possessions. Just list your main financial assets.

On the other side of the sheet, list all of your debts (liabilities). These include mortgages, student loans, credit card debt, and car loans—any money you owe to any person or institution.

Add up each column to see your total assets and your total liabilities.

Now, subtract your debts from your assets, and that's your net worth. It's positive if you own more than you owe, and vice versa.

As an alternative, use **Mint.com**, **Yodlee.com**, or similar programs to help you. You tell these programs what accounts you have at which financial institutions, give them your login and password for each, and the programs build you a net worth statement! They are always up-to-date, you can manually add accounts, and they represent a great option for tracking your net worth over time. I use both and love them. (I also know people who aren't comfortable giving all their usernames and passwords.)

Congratulations. You've done it. You now know where you stand financially in terms of financial wealth and cash flow. See—that didn't hurt.

Your Ideal Life

Now, on to the juicy part:

Part 1 is to figure what your ideal life costs.

Part 2 is to figure what it'll take to fund that for life.

Part 1: What does it cost to live your ideal life?

This question would certainly feel different if I had posed it at the beginning of the book. But after taking the time to clarify what matters most to you in life, you have no doubt gained an increased freedom from needing more money to be happier. You have a vision of a fulfilling life that requires money, but in that vision, your money is really supporting what you most care about, what most brings you alive.

Also, knowing that you are trading your life energy for money, you are likely more careful and intentional about your willingness to trade that energy.

"How much do I need?" is admittedly not an easy question. And the good news is that you don't have to have the complete answer right now—even a general sense is fine for now. There are a number of ways to start.

1. **Guess**. One option is to look at your current life and what you are spending and just declare, relative to that, how much you think it

would take to be living your ideal, thriving life. Again, your vision of thriving probably isn't about Ferraris—it more likely has to do with becoming who you know yourself capable of being, of being loving, or sharing meaningful experiences with people you love, of making a difference, and so on. So you might be able to just look at your life and, from a gut level, adjust what you currently spend. It might be up or down, but you might be able to just quickly say: I have a strong feeling that to thrive, love my life and have the money to fuel my adventure, it takes $X per year.

2. **Track and Adjust**. You might be using Quicken or Mint.com and be able to look at how much you are spending in various categories. Adjust those up or down based on how flexible that category is, and how much aliveness you are getting from each (in other words, how well your spending is "working" in that area—how much "return on spending" you are getting).

In any case, find your number! It'll change, so no need to be perfect and exact, but try to get well into the ballpark. Declare "I need $X per month (or per year) to live the life I'm being called to live!" Do it.

Part 2: Figuring out your Financial Freedom number:

If you want to wake up with the knowledge and confidence that you have a financial standing that is extremely likely to provide you with your desired spending for the rest of your life, you'll need the assets to do that.

Here, we are talking about either a pool of money from which you can draw (e.g., a portfolio), or an income "spigot" that is always on for you (e.g., pension, annuity, etc.).

In the simplest terms, if you have determined that you need $100K to live the life you want, and you estimate that $30K of that will be provided by a pension, then you are looking to generate $70K more a year from assets. In other words, you will need a pool of money that says "No worries, I can provide you $70K a year forever." Yes, I do mean increasing that for inflation each year.

Once you have an idea of what your desired spending is, we can figure out what pool of assets you'll need to sustain that.

Note that the pool you'll need depends on a number of variables. For example, are we talking about you needing this pool at age 40 or at 65? The pool needed is larger at age 40, because it will need to provide for you for a longer period of time.

Actually crunching the numbers requires a complex calculator that can account for tons of variables. This is another place in which I highly recommend getting some professional assistance.

That said, I want to offer some really good "shooting from the hip" help so that you can determine a ballpark number. (Lawyerly disclaimer: this is not a replacement for getting personalized professional advice. Use this for educational purposes only.)

The Safe Withdrawal Rate

The financial planning industry has done tons of research on the following question: How much can I draw from my portfolio when I retire? Whoever does the research and from whichever approach, the answers tend to be around the same: you can withdraw about 4–5%. Let's call it 4% to be safe.

They state that at retirement age (65), if you want to have a really high probability of a sustainable income that can be increased each year to keep pace with inflation, then you can take out (draw) about 4% of your portfolio in that first year.

This assumes a portfolio diversified between stocks and bonds, and it looks at all the periods in history over which someone might have drawn this percentage from the portfolio. It finds virtually no periods (historically) over which this would not have worked. There are some periods in which one could have safely drawn much more (say, 10%+), but 4% "ish" has been the maximum "safe" withdrawal rate. The research has much more complexity to it than this, but this is to give you a ballpark figure. (Again: future returns could be totally different from the past. Don't rely on this for certainty.) Based on this research, at retirement a $1 million portfolio should be able to offer about a $40,000 distribution per year (and be increased by inflation thereafter) based on a sustainable 4% draw.

To clarify, we're not talking about the investment income (e.g., stock dividend or bond interest or real estate rents) the portfolio is generating. Nor are we talking about the capital appreciation it earns. We're setting those concepts aside to simply point to how much money you can take out of a portfolio (regardless of its source). In reality, this method typically ends up using some yield and some appreciation.

Next, hang with a little math here: 4% is $1/25^{th}$ of 100, right? Put differently: $100 = 25 \times 4$. Why did I just get numbery on you?

Because this helps us see that the amount of money you need saved at retirement is roughly twenty five times your annual spending.

Or, if we use 5% as the safe withdrawal rate, then that's $1/20^{th}$ of 100 ($20 \times 5 = 100$) and thus it takes twenty times our annual spending at retirement to fund our lifestyle (that is, to allow for the 5% withdrawal).

So, this is saying it takes assets of around twenty or thirty times our annual spending at retirement to have the pool of money needed to be financially free. Call it thirty times if you are concerned and conservative, or younger.

If you spend $100K a year, it'll take $2 million to $2.5 million (to $3 million) to fund that $100K annual spending.

We're being simplistic, but this is a really great first step in giving you an idea of what kind of net worth it takes to have financial freedom.

If you need the pool for longer (because you retire earlier) then you need a larger pool—perhaps thirty times your annual spending.

And, of course, if part of your income need is already provided for by a pension, social security, passive business, etc., then you need less. If you expect your investments to earn more than the researchers assumed in their research (and I'd be averse to doing that), then you'd need less money, and vice versa.

Without making this a full finance lecture, here you have the heart of it. Assuming no other income sources, you'll need to have somewhere between twenty and thirty times your annual spending saved up to have financial freedom. That savings can have lots of forms (portfolio, business, real estate, etc.), but this should give you a rough idea.

All of this assumes smooth, regular spending, but you might have bumps (e.g., daughter's wedding, a big trip, etc.). You'll need additional amounts saved for extra expenses of relatively short duration. Paying for college is a great example. The 4% withdrawal rate doesn't account for those extras, and you need to plan for those as well.

Finally, the 4% withdrawal rate assumes that your asset is one from which you can withdraw. Your home typically is not such an asset. There are ways to get money out of a home, but in this safe withdrawal rate discussion, we're talking mainly about having assets whose value is accessible and can be withdrawn. Many people hold illiquid assets—those should not be counted unless there is a plan for making them liquid.

These can better be accounted for with a more detailed analysis. Contact me at **Colin@DrakeWealth.com** if you want to discuss doing this—it's fun and super enlightening.

The Lever:

In all the years of helping people crunch numbers, plan for financial independence, and understand their overall financial picture, the most surprising thing for them has consistently been the impact that their level of spending has on their financial plan. If you need to have, say, twenty-five times your annual spending saved at retirement, that means every dollar you feel you need to support your retirement lifestyle requires that you saved up $25 along the way. For every $10,000 more you feel you need to spend annually in retirement, that translates to $250,000 more you will need to have built up.

When I crunch numbers with clients, they are typically shocked to see that working an extra year has little effect on their financial plan, whereas increasing spending by $20K a year has a big impact. That's because the extra year of income is one "drop" into the bucket, whereas the $20K a year spending is an annual draw from the bucket for over thirty years. It has a MUCH bigger impact. They need roughly $500K more to allow for that.

It's like a lever; for every little bit you push down on one side (e.g., $1) the other side goes up by a large amount (e.g., $25).

This is sometimes scary, but no worries. You can do this. You can figure out how much you really need to thrive, how much it takes for financial independence and how to create that.

Enough

Here's an extremely powerful question in our quest for wealth: How much is *ENOUGH?*

How much do you really need; how much is enough to live a thriving life? I'm not going to offer answers, but simply point out that this question can change your life.

This question may feel in contrast to the dreaming of having-it-all exercises we've done in Chapter 6. You might see it that way, or you might see it as an improvement upon the vision. That's up to you.

In many ways, isn't "enough" the "ideal"? If you are really clear about what your ideal life is, then "enough" is just right—what's the point of more? More than ideal? Is there such a thing? Isn't that "too muchness," and isn't that worse than "ideal."

Vicki Robin and Joe Dominguez wrote a great book called *Your Money or Your Life*, and I highly recommend it. She's the queen of "enoughness" and offers hearty wisdom in the quest to balance life with money.

We live in a culture of "more," and the trap we can fall into is that of never being satisfied. Until we have our own answer for how much is enough, we'll always be at risk of pursuing more. And pursuing more can easily come at the risk of delivering less. Perhaps the refinement comes in the question "How much is enough to *thrive?"*

> *"Enough is as good as a feast."*
>
> **English Proverb**

I've got a friend who sold a tech company for millions. He never needs to work another day in his life. Yet what's he doing with his time? Trying to go out and make more money. Without clarity about his "enough" point, and without listening for his calling, he just keeps on doing what he's comfortable with: seeking prestige and money. He's a great guy—he just hasn't found his Sweet Spot or his enough point.

For many years, Jerry Seinfeld was the highest-paid man in television. That's because his show, *Seinfeld*, was making a fortune for NBC. Former NBC president Warren Littlefield recalls heading over to meet with Jerry to cut a deal for the next season. Warren's NBC colleagues kept wondering why Warren was so worried about Jerry not taking the deal. "Warren—we're putting $110 million on the table for Jerry. There's *no way* he's *not* going to take it. Relax!" they told him.

But Warren knew something they didn't: Jerry didn't have a life. He was pouring all his heart and soul, time and energy, into the show, was constantly at the studio, and was finally noticing that he didn't have a wife, kids, time with friends, etc. Warren put the $110 million on the table and Jerry Seinfeld did something amazing. He said, "No thanks." He had hit his "enough" point and virtually no amount of money was going to keep him from the other kind of wealth he was seeking. Thus ended the show *Seinfeld* (and thus started Seinfeld's family).

ACTION

Write the word "enough?" on the palm of your hand each day this week. Let it spark the inquiry in you about how much is enough. Ask it about the big picture of life and of the concrete thing in front of you, like lunch. What happens when you eat too much, work too much, or complain too much? How nice a car is enough? How many nights out at a restaurant is enough?

Wealth consists not in having great possessions, but in having few wants.

Epictetus

So, by now you have a clear picture of your cash flow and your net worth, you have somewhat of an idea of your ideal lifestyle (and will ponder the question: how much is enough) and you have a rough tool for figuring how much you need to be financially free (and you are going to get professional help getting a more specific answer).

You've just defined Point A and Point B on your Woohoo! Wealth Graph. Congratulations. You know where you are and roughly where you want to be.

Now, isn't that more helpful than living in fog about it? You might be thinking: "How am I going to build that wealth?" Especially if your Woohoo! is weak, and so are your savings. But at least you are clearer about the game and your target. And next we'll turn to answering your question.

To sum up: Get in the game! Know your numbers. Take control. You've got to know your numbers, and it can even be fun and inspiring. Your path to creating financial freedom requires that you get clear about exactly what that means numerically to you. It's pretty easy, so go for it. (Do you hold a belief about numbers that's an obstacle? "I suck at numbers," or "This is way too complicated"? Find it, tear it out, replace it with "I can totally do this—I'm on it! Woohoo!")

CHAPTER 9

Pillar #5:
Have a "Sweet Spot" Wealth-Building Plan

Most people don't have a specific plan, a chosen method for building wealth. They aren't clear about how they are going to make the money!

You may know where you are headed, but if you don't know how you are going to get there, what are the chances that you'll get there? If you can't explain exactly how you intend to build financial wealth, what are the chances you will? Isn't that a plan based on hope and luck?

> **There are only a handful of ways to build wealth and you need to pick (at least) one to use.**

By now, you are clearer about what you want in life and the role money does and doesn't play in getting that. You are clearer about your obstacles. You know where you stand financially in terms of net worth and cash flow. You have an idea of what your ideal lifestyle costs you and how much you are going to need saved up to sustain that from passive income.

Now, it's time to figure out HOW you will do that.

For some people, this is where it gets scary because of three beliefs about building assets:

1. I don't know *how* I'm going to do it.

2. I don't believe that I *can* do it.

3. I believe I'm going to *suffer* doing it.

It's understandable that these would be stressful beliefs. But the solution provides the antidote. The solution: Find your *Sweet Spot*, deliver massive *value*, and *build wealth* from it.

We're going to lay a little more groundwork before diving into exploring the specific methods of building wealth.

> *"My mother said to me, 'If you become a soldier, you'll be a general, if you become a monk you'll end up as the pope.' Instead, I became a painter and wound up as Picasso."*
>
> **Pablo Picasso**

Your Sweet Spot

Here's a little formula for you:

Sweet Spot = Strengths + Passion + Impact

As I described earlier, when you find people who are thriving, they tend to be using their greatest **strengths**, applying them towards something about which they are **passionate,** and making an **impact** that they find meaningful. These people are leading engaged, purposeful, meaningful lives. They're giving their best for the good of others, and loving it! They know their *what* and their *why* in life.

These are the people others call "amazing" because they are just so damned good at what they do and seem to love it so much. And we think what they are doing is just great. I know you know these folks. Your job is to BE one of these folks.

I just watched the play *The Music Man* in an outdoor amphitheater on our local mountain, Mount Tamalpais. There was a section for the hearing impaired, and for three hours, this wonderful woman full of sassy character translated the play into sign language. She was so fun, and funny, and animated. You could tell she loved it, and her audience loved her. I left thinking, "She's amazing!" She's in her Sweet Spot—using her gifts towards something about which she is passionate, making a difference and getting to freely express the best of herself in the process.

The ultimate thing you can do to build your *personal* wealth, your fulfillment, your Woohoo!, is to find your Sweet Spot. That's where you come alive and love your life.

The ultimate thing you can do to build your <u>*financial*</u> wealth is to find your Sweet Spot and **deliver massive value that is in demand.** That's where you love your life and people pay you well for the value you deliver.

That key to building wealth can thus be added into this same equation:

Sweet Spot *Wealth* = Strengths + Passion + *Valued* Impact in *DEMAND*

When you are using your strengths towards your passion and making an impact that is something of *value* that is in *demand*, then you have a fabulous wealth-building condition. This means people want what you offer and are willing to pay you for it.

The fastest way to building wealth is to deliver massive value to the world.

I'll illustrate with some examples: If your strength, passion and impact happens to be in the area of rehabilitating injured duck-billed platypuses (technically, it's platypodes. But, c'mon—you would have said "what's a platypode?", right?) you can create a lot of Woohoo! in your life by dedicating yourself to it. But this is something that is neither highly *valued* in our world nor highly in *demand*. So, pursuing that is a good recipe for enjoying life, but not a good one for building wealth.

You might be someone who is passionate about teaching children sports, yet your days are spent as an investment banker, a job you dislike but which generates massive income. Good plan for accumulating assets, poor plan for enjoying life. (Yeah, I know… you can sock away a bunch then quit. Good for you.)

The magic ingredient to building wealth is to have demand for the value (or impact) you are passionate about creating.

Do What You Love and…

You know the saying… "Do what you love and the money will follow." The money will probably *not* follow if what you love is the duck-billed platypus. "Do what you love *that creates massive value that is in demand*, and the money will follow" is more like it.

The greater the value you create and the greater the demand for it, the greater your wealth.

You can create something of small value (e.g., a $1 toy, a book) that is in massive demand by millions and create wealth. (Hello, Harry Potter. Hello, Beanie Babies.)

You can build one thing of high value (a business for example) that has the demand to be bought and create wealth that way. (Hello, Facebook.)

Or you can create something of modest value with modest demand and create value over time. (Dry cleaning, anyone?)

The point is that you must create value for which others are willing to exchange money.

Wealth-Building Potential = Value x Demand

> *"Whoever renders service to many puts himself in line for greatness—great wealth, great return, great satisfaction, great reputation, and great joy."*
>
> **Jim Rohn**

ACTION

So far in your life, how much value have you created, and how much demand has there been for it?

Let's look a little more closely at the **Sweet Spot**:

Your Strengths

You have a unique set of strengths. Nobody looks at the world quite the way you do. Nobody has had your experiences. There are things about you that nobody in the world can offer the way you do. Some of your strengths are natural gifts, while others you have cultivated.

The world is not looking for you to fix your weaknesses. The world is begging for you to use your strengths for its betterment. YOU are the ONE for some job (whatever that is).

The world has a terrible misallocation of human capital. We have so many of the wrong people in the wrong jobs. How many people do you know who *adore* their work, who give it their all, and are in the perfect career for them? How many of your friends would you say this about: "Oh—you are SO perfect for that job. That is SO you!"? Probably a minority.

It's so common to start a career that balances our interest in it with our need for money. Then we get used to it, get used to the money, get comfortable and then just keep on keeping on. We don't stop and take measure of how much we love what we do, how much it draws on our greatest gifts and how much we give a damn about the result of our efforts.

Wouldn't it stand to reason that your financial success is more likely to be fueled by you using your greatest strengths? By you doing what you are really great at? By doing what you love to do?

Well, what are your greatest strengths? If people were to pick the *one* thing they would most come to you for, what might they say? Can you declare with great pride and certainty what your strengths are? Do you know what your unique abilities are?

Now might also be a good time to check on any limiting belief that might be holding you back: "I can't make money with my strengths," or "I don't really have any strengths," or "others might get lucky enough to earn a living using their strengths, but it's not in the cards for me." Got anything like this going on? Zap it. Claim the opposite as your truth! You want to do something totally amazing and fun? Figure that out!

ACTION

Perhaps one of the most powerful and fun ways to get clear about your strengths is to *ask other people* what they are. Others will *love* to help you figure this out. It's a feel-good-fest.

How can you do that? Just ask people, "What would you say are my greatest strengths?"

Whoa! Does that sound hard to do? Well then, preface it with something like, "I'm in the middle of reading this fantastic book called *Woohoo! Wealth,* and I'm doing an exercise to get clearer about what my greatest strengths are. It's part of a strategy for building wealth and aliveness. Would you be willing to help me by offering me your perspective on what you see as my greatest strengths?"

You might ask questions like:
- What do you see as my unique combination of strengths?
- What am I good at?
- What would you come to me for help with?
- What does it seem to you that I love?
- What would be the perfect job for me?
- What do you see being important to me?
- What do you see me *doing* that gets results?
- Who do you see me *being* when I'm at my best?

You can write people a letter or email with these questions or ask them to have a conversation with you. Offer to give them time to consider it. You aren't asking for feedback about how to fix your weaknesses—you are asking where and how you shine. Do it—it's a blast, and it will thrill you and deepen your connection with the people you ask. Just put aside your modesty and ask! Offer to return the favor (and have them read this book for context).

Take your collected answers and distill them for the heart of it. What's the core? What's so YOU about you? What are your unique strengths, your special gifts, your signature abilities?

That's what the world wants from you!

Everybody just told you that. There—you have your answer!

I have mine figured out. Want to hear it? I have the unique ability to create a safe space in which people want to come alive. I bring a refreshing combination of head and heart, of financial expertise and life wisdom. I am a call to aliveness and a method for creating it. I am an inspirational wealth planner. That's the work I do. And I love it.

What's yours? Make a statement out of it. Own it. Anything less is wasting the best of you.

What else can you do to better know your strengths?

- Contemplate that question in nature.
- Take a personal-growth workshop on the topic.
- Try reading *StrengthsFinder 2.0* by Tom Rath (**www.strengthsfinder.com**). He has an online test that summarizes your greatest strengths.
- Read *Now, Discover Your Strengths* by Marcus Buckingham & Donald Clifton.
- Take personality tests such as the Myers–Briggs (**www.myersbriggs.org**), Kolbe (**www.Kolbe.com**) or the Enneagram (**www.enneagraminstitute.com**).
- Google "find your strengths," and you'll find tons on the topic.

Just dive in and keep getting clearer. Know the best you have to offer the world. Then deliver tons of value. That's a recipe for wealth. Go for it!

In our culture, there's a lot of emphasis on trying to improve our weaknesses. It's well validated now that that's not nearly as effective as using our strengths, while having a system to get support with our weak areas.

The same goes for organizations. The field of Appreciative Inquiry has demonstrated that it's much less effective to ask "What's wrong, and how can we fix it?" than it is to ask "What's working well, and how can we get more of that?"

The way you frame your questions and place your focus has enormous power in your quest for success. Focus on your strengths.

Your Passions

"Sometimes success is due less to ability than to zeal."

Charles Buxton

Knowing your strengths is only part of the equation. Knowing what to apply them towards is another. I have strengths that would make me a great psychologist, and others that would make me an excellent financial analyst, but I'm not passionate about either.

It matters where you apply your strengths. And it matters most for two reasons: When you apply your strengths towards something you love…

1. It gives you energy and endurance.
2. You engage.

Energy, endurance, and engagement are great qualities for helping you create wealth and for living a great life.

"Believe with all of your heart that you will do what you were made to do."

Orison Swett Marden

The word passion might well be at the very heart of what Woohoo! Wealth is all about. Passion is aliveness. When you are passionate about something, it brings you alive. We often associate the word passion with sexual passion. Arousal. And that's beautiful—isn't sexual arousal a powerful form of aliveness, of having energy coursing through your body, of having life force?

And in this context of building wealth, we apply our strengths towards something about which we are passionate. That means it's actually what we *do*. It's how we spend our *time*. And that means it's how we spend our *life*. So, it's extremely important to choose wisely—our life depends upon it.

"Dost thou love life? Then do not squander time, for that is the stuff life is made of."

Benjamin Franklin

And, for a far-out thought, human evolution depends upon it. Those courageously and innovatively giving their best towards their passions drive the forefront of evolution. It's people in their Sweet Spots who are pushing the boundaries in all fields (scientific, athletic, business, etc.). They are the game changers, the front-runners who are literally shaping the course of human evolution. Steve Jobs, Albert Einstein, Mother Teresa, and Gandhi were all people in their Sweet Spots who changed the course of human evolution by passionately applying their greatest gifts to change the world.

Not only does your life depend upon you finding your Sweet Spot, our species does too!!! In fact, maybe all species depend on us finding our Sweet Spots.

Permission for Passion

There are two main reasons people don't live their passions:

1. They aren't sure what their passion is.

2. They know, but just don't feel permission to pursue it.

That last one sounds strange. But it's very common. We can feel like we don't deserve it, or like life is not supposed to be that sweet, or that it would be too good to be true. We can too quickly believe that we couldn't support ourselves if we allowed ourselves to live our passion. Some of us fear success and greatness, others the vulnerability of failure in pursuing our passion.

You've got to dream! Let yourself feel and admit what you are passionate about. The number one thing that prevents us from dreaming and connecting with our passion is this: that voice that comes into our head and says, "Well that's great that you love nature, but how the hell are you going to make a living at it? Pick another more reasonable passion." And we do! We listen to that goddamned voice and it zaps our passion right out of us.

> *"Don't ask what the world needs. Ask what makes you come alive and go do that. Because what the world needs is more people who have come alive."*
>
> **Howard Thurman**

To connect with what you are passionate about, you have to allow yourself time to dream and search in a "critic-free zone." Tell that voice to get the hell out of here, to go grab a coffee and come back when you are done!

Whatever the case, if you want to live your passion, you've got to know it, choose it, allow it, and go for it. Do you have a better idea? Strive for the life of tepid interest, of lukewarm engagement, of somewhat amusing pastimes?

You are either going to spend your life doing what you love, or you aren't. The choice is yours. The Woohoo! Wealth community is full of people who have declared, "I'm in. I'm totally committed to knowing my passions and doing my best to earn my living from them. It's where I'll have my best to give to the world and thus my best chance of creating value and being financially rewarded for it." How about you—are you in? I know—it's not easy. Still, the only real thing likely to be in your way is that voice saying you can't.

Perhaps what you love isn't something that lends itself to making a living. If that's the case, then the question is, how can I have plenty of time for my passion while I make a living doing something else I love?

Your Impact

"You make a living by what you earn; you make a life by what you give."

Winston Churchill

It's all well and good to give your best to something you love, but if it doesn't make any difference to you or the world, what's the point? Or what if it makes a difference, but you don't particularly care about the difference it makes? You could be a hairstylist who is fantastic at her job, loves it, and revels in boosting her clients' well-being and confidence. Or you might be great at it, love it, but feel like it doesn't really matter that much what people's hair looks like. Neither one is right; it's a matter of how important your impact is to *you*, given your values and view of the world.

Most people seek meaning from what they *do*, and that typically comes from seeing that their efforts make a difference that matters to *them*. The guy helping the platypus clearly feels great about making a difference in that one life. You might not find it important.

You hold strong values about what's important in life and what isn't. When your work supports what matters, then you enjoy meaning from your work.

Further, there are degrees of impact. You can make an impact on a very small and local scale. You might, for example, be a fantastic cook, passionate about great tacos, and be making a small local impact with your taco truck. Or you might be making an impact on a massive scale. You might be passionate about green building and be making an international impact with your designs, lectures and teachings.

The absolute size of your impact isn't as important as the size of the impact you are making relative to your potential and your values. You want to feel challenged, like you are stretching and fulfilling your potential. Then again, you don't want to sacrifice family and health in the process. There's a Sweet Spot for impact, too—not too big, not too small—just right.

And it's also possible that the impact you want to have doesn't involve other people; you may just want to create for your own joy, or you may want to impact forests. The point is that most people want to do something that says, "I was here in the world."

Pillar #2 focused on discovering what you really want in life. Your Sweet Spot is about marrying what you want in life with what you want to *do* and *give*. Your Sweet Spot is about discovering your purpose and living it.

> *"I honestly think it is better to be a failure at something you love than to be a success at something you hate."*
>
> **George Burns**

The world is full of great books and programs on discovering your life purpose, and also full of coaches and guides who are here to help with that. Here, I will offer one exercise I've found powerful. To do it, find a quiet place where you can close your eyes and reflect. While driving is perfect (just kidding).

Read the following, then close your eyes and see yourself in that situation. Discover what answers come up for you.

ACTION

There you are, backstage. You can hear the full auditorium abuzz with excitement as the seats fill up. The energy is high and hopeful. There is much anticipation in the air. In a few moments, you are going to be on stage before this audience. They are here to see you! And thrilled about it.

And here's the best part… this is a magical evening: you have been bestowed with the ability to have *any* impact you wish on this audience. They will experience the impact or transformation that you intend for them. Guaranteed. They will leave the auditorium changed in whatever way you decide.

Close your eyes now and imagine yourself ready to come out on stage. To great applause, you bound onto the stage and begin speaking to your people.

What do you talk about? What is the magical impact you have on them? What is the transformation they experience?

Well done. What did you come up with? What's the difference you want to make? If you could have any impact on the world, what would it be?

If you look at your answer carefully, you are very likely to find your life's purpose, that which you feel is the most important use of your time and energy during your time on earth.

What, in your heart, do you feel simply *must* happen in the world? What has to get done? What do you know you are the right person to take on?

Alternately, what *must* stop in the world, in your community, or in institutions? What drives you crazy about the world that you want to do something about? What riles you up or breaks your heart?

For example, did you know that every 3.6 seconds a baby dies of hunger/malnutrition in our world. A *baby!* *DEAD!* A dozen have died while you read this paragraph. A further 24,000 will die today. Almost 9 million will die this year. (Statistics vary, but it's millions and millions.)

That breaks my heart, yet it's not my mission. Is it yours?

One of my teachers, Martin Siesta, once said to me:

"When you find the conversation you want to be in in life, you've found your calling."

This had a tremendous impact on me. I used that to assess the conversation I was in with clients and saw that it was over-focused on the dollars and sense. What I really wanted to talk about was how to live a fantastic life and how to create powerful finances to fuel that. So, I set out to change the conversation I was in. And I've found my calling.

What's the conversation you want to be in?

"You're happiest while you're making the greatest contribution."
Robert F. Kennedy

Maybe that simple exercise clarified your life purpose. Perhaps not at all. In either case, the purpose of raising the topic is to make this point…

Your Sweet Spot is the one in which you are living your life's purpose.

And, in building wealth, you have a massive resource of energy, drive, creativity, and passion when working from your Sweet Spot.

Find your Sweet Spot! Claim it! It's yours, and it's just sitting there waiting for you.

> *"The key to success is to raise your own energy. When you do, people will naturally be attracted to you. And when they show up, bill 'em."*
>
> **Stuart Wilde**

Building Financial Wealth

OK. Here you stand with greater clarity about (1) what you want in life, (2) what your strengths are, (3) what your passions are, (4) what impact you find meaningful, and (5) what your purpose is.

This is the platform upon which you will build your wealth. Any other way is inferior. Any other is at the cost of your aliveness, and thus, literally, your life.

There will always be ways to make more money, but this is the way to make the most LIFE. And that's what you want the money for anyway!

OK. Now that we've laid some more groundwork, back to the HOW of it all…

Your Human Capital

When you built your net worth statement, you looked around your financial life and counted every asset you could actually see. That is, if you had a bank account, you counted that. If you had a brokerage account, you added that in.

There's another "invisible" asset to consider when assessing your financial life and planning to build wealth. That asset, your *human capital*, is the *present value* of all of the money you will ever earn in the future.

To illustrate the concept of present value, consider this example: If you knew that a friend was going to give you $100 on January 1 for the next five years, what would that be worth to you *today?* The answer is a bit less than $500 (say, $420). The reason it's less than the full $500 is because of something called the *time value of money,* which basically states that money in your hand today is worth more than money received in the future. Future money gets "discounted."

With that explained, each of us who is out earning money in the world has a *present value* of all of our future income. You might think of human capital as current wealth *potential.* You can calculate how much that's worth today.

For example:

- A 25-year-old earning $50,000 a year, whose salary simply keeps pace with inflation until retirement age, has a present value of that future salary of about $1,200,000.
- A 40-year-old earning $150,000 a year until age 65 (again, keeping pace with inflation) has a current value of human capital of about $2.7 million.

- A 65-year-old about to retire has virtually no human capital left if she plans never to work for money again.

What's important about human capital? **It may be your most valuable financial asset!** The younger you are, the more likely it is that this human capital is your largest financial asset. That's because you've had less time to build up actual dollars, and you have more years of earning ahead of you.

Clearly, we can't be too precise in quantifying the value of your human capital, because so many factors will contribute to changing how much you earn and for how long. Therein, however, also lies the beauty of this concept called human capital. You have the ability to influence the value of your human capital by the decisions you make. Simply put, the higher your potential earning and the longer your potential earning, the more valuable your current human capital.

I sometimes see people in their 30s or 40s putting tons of effort into trying to increase return on a relatively modest portfolio. The reality is that they would be better served tending to their much more valuable asset: Their human capital! Their portfolio may be worth $150,000, while their human capital may be worth $1,500,000, yet they aren't tending to that human capital.

How do you tend to human capital? The answer is to do anything that increases:

- The *amount* of money you can earn.
- The rate at which you can *increase* your earnings.
- The *duration* for which you can earn money.
- The *certainty* with which you will earn money.

What would some examples be?

- Invest in education that increases the value of your knowledge and skills. That's almost always a good return on investment.
- Do work you love and want to continue doing longer.
- Work in a career that has high potential income growth.
- Play an active role in increasing your earning (e.g., renegotiate salary, change companies, deliver more value).
- Start a business.
- Strengthen your position (value) within an organization.

Your human capital is the wealth that's already *theoretically* in the pipeline. And, this *potential* wealth is what you are going to convert and use to build your *real* wealth. The more *potential* wealth you have in the pipeline, the more *real* wealth you can materialize.

ACTION

What do you think the value of your human capital is? For a rough estimate (ignoring discounting), just tally up all your potential future earnings over the rest of your life. Make a list of the specific ways in which you could increase the value of your human capital.

The Various Methods of Building Wealth

In the simplest terms, your ultimate financial goal is to maximize your human capital, convert it to real capital and then build a "money machine," one that provides you with the income you need to live your ideal life, predictably, securely and sustainably. Right? You just want to "go to the mailbox and collect your check." As long as there is some mechanism providing that for you, you are good to go.

So the question then becomes, how do I build a money machine? One of two ways:

1. Build it steadily over time by saving and investing.

2. Build it in big chunks by creating and selling something of value.

There are only a handful of ways to create financial wealth. It's going to be important for your financial life planning that you emerge with a plan that includes the specific method you intend to use to build your wealth. That's much more likely to get you there than, "Um, I'm not sure."

Let's look at the main methods of building wealth…

Earn and Save:

This is the one most people are familiar with, and the most common form of this one is to hold a job (though this includes self-employment too).

In this method of building wealth, you expect to earn a steady stream of income over a long period of time. Examples would be a teacher, a doctor, a ferryboat captain, an accountant, or an engineer—jobs where you have a fairly predictable pay scale and aren't likely to see anything deviate too substantially from that scale.

In this method of building wealth, you spend less than you earn and save the difference. Those savings accumulate, typically in investments such as stocks, bonds, and real estate, and the goal is to accumulate enough to reach your financial freedom number.

Build and Sell:

In this form of building wealth, your earnings come mainly from building something of value, and then selling it. This could include real estate development, business building, or inventing. The key here is that you typically put most of your resources into creating something that didn't exist before and which will be considered valuable to others. You create value from thin air. That value is most often derived from the cash flow the buyer expects to enjoy from owning your creation or from their expectation to resell it at a higher price.

Without a doubt, this has forever been the most powerful wealth-building method available. Look at the Forbes 400 list of the world's wealthiest people; it's chock full of billionaires who built something of value and sold it (or enjoy massive income from it). The same goes for your run-of-the-mill millionaires—most have created wealth through owning a business.

Be a Broker:

Deals need to get done and there are always people in the middle of deals. Real estate brokers; investment bankers; international commodities brokers. These people put two sides together, handle the details, and take their commission. The greater the size of the deals, the greater the wealth-building opportunities.

Invest:

Investors buy into other businesses, deals or projects, or lend them money. In exchange, they expect a return on their investment. Speculators tend to seek big wins and are willing to take big risks. Investors tend to seek steady, longer-term growth. Venture capitalists seek companies in their infancy that are ready to skyrocket. Private Equity folks look to buy businesses, improve them and resell them. These are all forms of investment.

Be a Star:

There are the lucky few whose talent, looks and abilities catapult them into the national or global limelight and whose brand commands massive earnings. Brad Pitt, Kobe Bryant, Madonna, and Kim Kardashian are examples. If you have something about you (talent, looks, lifestyle, allure) craved by millions, you might have the opportunity to monetize that and become wealthy.

Get Lucky:

Inheritors, lottery winners, gamblers, landowners with oil below—any of these can leave you very wealthy without having had much to do with it.

Create Art:

Think Beatles, Jackson Pollock, Steven Spielberg, or Jean-Paul Gaultier. If you create something which will either offer you a one-time massive sum (e.g., a painting) or a long stream of royalties or licensing fees (e.g., music royalties, perfume licensing fees, movie action figure sales, etc.), you can make a fortune with that.

Be a Criminal:

You can steal money, extort, scam, or sue for it; or sell drugs, weapons, or stolen vehicles, etc. Hey—it's actually a massive part of the world economy and an enormous creator of wealth for some. But let's skip this one.

Possibility times Probability:

OK. So which methods of building wealth work best or fastest, and which should you use?

A powerful way to look at this question is to consider how much money you can make and how likely are you to make that? In other words, to consider the possible **range of earnings** for each method while considering their **probability**.

Let's take **Stardom** for example. People setting out to become famous athletes or actors have the potential for massive earnings, yet have a dismal probability of success. This is the equivalent of buying a career lottery ticket. That's not to say that you can't make a wonderful life full of security and aliveness by pursuing your art—it's just very unlikely to build big financial wealth for you.

Thus, you have a range of making anywhere between zero dollars and hundreds of millions of dollars on this wealth creation path, but the likelihood of millions is tiny. In fact, I've heard it said that 96% of all money paid to actors gets paid to the top thirty actors. The remaining 4% is split among all the rest.

Let's look at the **Earning and Saving method**. If you are a teacher, you can pretty clearly see the income potential for your specialty. Google "First Grade Teacher Salary Range," and you'll quickly find that the national range is between $30K and $60K a year. You won't find any first grade teachers earning $700K a year.

The probability of earning between $30K and $60K is very high, and the possibility of earning ten times that is extremely low.

It's clear that the route to building wealth in that career is to spend less than you earn, and to save the difference and live modestly. Then invest and let time and compound interest work their magic.

If your job is one in which the possibility of earnings is in the $500K to $1 million range, and the probability of you achieving that is relatively high (oh, say, investment banker or hedge-fund manager), then this job can allow you huge potential to save money. You aren't building something to sell, but your income is so high that you've got tons of potential to save big money.

Let's look at **Build and Sell**. If you start or buy a business, what's the possible outcome: Zero to billions. You can lose your shirt in a startup that runs out of money, or you can create a little website called Facebook and make billions.

What about the likelihood of success? We hear statistics that most businesses fail in their first five years. That means it's not likely. But it's done all the time, is certainly a good possibility, and is quite possibly your best bet at building something that creates a high income, a high sales value, or both. Most people who become wealthy do so owning their own business. That says an enormous amount. The basic recipe for success is: see what others have done and model them.

Let's look at **Brokering.** If you are a residential real estate agent in a modest, crowded and "cool" market, you're not likely to earn a huge income. If you are one of the few people who can broker a deal to build hydroelectric dams, you're likely to be able to get a big chunk for your slice of those deals.

The point is, when considering *how* to build wealth, you must apply the very important questions:

What's the earning potential?

What's the probability of earning that?

ACTION

Take a look at what you are doing to earn money right now. What's the possible range of earnings you could enjoy in your work? What's the probability that you will be on the high end of the range? Take a good look. This might be the first time you realize that you're never going to build wealth doing what you are currently doing. Or you might find tons of potential. This first step is to clearly assess your current wealth-building potential on the basis of possibility and probability.

Can You Scale Your Income?

And here's a great way to help you assess that possibility and probability: Ask yourself how much *harder* work, *smarter* work, or *leveraged* work have the potential to pay off more. In other words, how much *scalability* exists?

When a first-grade teacher works a lot harder, that doesn't change their income potential much, does it? When a salesman works harder, he can potentially see a corresponding increase in his pay. When a business owner works harder, smarter, and uses leverage—their earnings theoretically become unlimited. Using leverage means using other people's time, energy, talent or money to amplify your results.

ACTION

Look at what you are currently doing to earn money. Assess whether working harder, smarter or using leverage is likely to result in commensurately higher earnings.

Creating Your Game Plan

So how do you apply all this? Ask: What's your game plan? There's no right or wrong. There's just more or less likely to build wealth, more or less potential compensation, more or less scalability, and more or less Sweet Spot.

If I could wish upon you anything in this area, it would be this:

To know what you want, to be clear about what your Sweet Spot is, and to find a highly profitable, probable and scalable way to deliver your gifts. I want you to love your work and to have great earning potential. I want your harder and smarter work to pay you more. That's what I'd like you to figure out how to do. In fact—I challenge you to do it.

You can scale back on that wish, but if you do, it all starts to compromise your optimal living.

What would that look like for you? Imagine it. What would be absolutely fantastic? Design it. What can you do with your life that will allow you to feel wealthy (alive!) as you build financial wealth? What could you be doing now that is what you'd be doing anyway, once you had the money?

Remember that we started this book with "The Parable of the Mexican Fisherman"?

How can the work you do be essentially what you would do with your life if you didn't need the money?

I say: Start *there!* Figure out how to do that. That's a life well lived. Just as the fisherman is living well, how can you do that?

If you are going to take a job with a relatively predictable and somewhat modest salary, be clear: you've got to choose the Earn and Save path. And then you've got to save! Please hear this message loudly: You aren't going to create wealth with your job unless you save money and build assets with those savings.

That's the reality of it. And it's a core reason 99% of people don't become financially wealthy. Because they have modest-income jobs and save virtually nothing.

Want to be wealthy? Don't be one of them.

Want to have a job? Relatively few people who work for others become wealthy. Get good at saving, at living below your means. Know your numbers. Work with a planner to estimate how much you need to save per month, year or paycheck. Get on track to building the wealth you want in order to be financially free. It won't be easy, but it's doable. Millions have done it.

Doing nothing, or just winging it, is a recipe for failure. Be really clear about that. Am I sugar-coating it enough?

If you are inclined to build wealth more quickly, then it makes a lot of sense to consider what business you can start or buy that allows you to work in your Sweet Spot, and which has a high potential earning, a reasonable probability of succeeding and scalability.

Being an entrepreneur is your most likely route to building wealth. Think about it this way. **For you to have "big money," somebody is going to have to give it to you, right? And they are going to want something from you for it. What do they want? To make money!** So to the extent that you can build a machine that makes money, others will be happy to pay you for it. They'll pay you in proportion to the predictability of making money, to the systemization of the money machine, and to the likely endurance of that machine.

If I had a money machine I wanted to sell you, and it kicked out a steady $100 a day, every day, without fail and without requiring your participation, how much would you be willing to pay for that machine? (Business valuation experts could help you figure out exactly what to pay for it.) Now, if that machine kicked out anywhere from $25 to $150 most, but not all days, took a lot of tinkering and looked like it might break in a year or two, how much would you pay for that machine? Much less, obviously.

The people who have the money and are going to want to give it to you are looking to buy money machines. ATMs. Build one and they will come. Make it systematized, solid, predictable, easy, and independent of you and your skills, and they will pay you more for it.

Investors buy revenue streams (or revenue potential), or they buy something they plan to resell for more money later (e.g., a painting, raw land).

While that doesn't tell you exactly what *you* are going to do to build wealth, it lays an important foundation for thinking it through.

ACTION

Take a look at your current life and assess:

Am I trying to build something and sell it? Or to build something and enjoy great income from it? Or am I trying to earn money and save it?

What am I doing? What's my game plan?

Picture yourself in front of a panel of wise, successful and "vicious" wealthy business people. You are about to pitch them your strategy for creating wealth. Would you stand proudly and confidently declaring your wealth plan, or would you want to run away?

If you haven't created a reasonable, realistic, and probable way of building assets, then you won't build assets.

Part of your wealth-building strategy must be to **declare your asset accumulation game plan**.

There are a million ways it can look. For example:

> *"My strategy is to keep working at the university where I have tenure. I love teaching. It's my Sweet Spot. I have a salary of $120,000, I save $25,000 a year, already have $1.5 million saved, and calculations suggest that I'm on a great track to hit my target asset goal of $3 million while I'm in my early 60s. Woohoo!"*

Or...

> *"My goal is to grow this business I adore to revenues of $4 million, with a bottom line profit of $1 million; to ensure everything is systematized, scalable, and transferrable; and to seek a buyer offering a multiple of 1–2 times revenue in the next seven years. Woohoo!"*

Or…

"I need to do three deals in the next seven years, each netting me $2 million, to hit my financial freedom number. I can do that."

Or…

"I need 250 members for my Cross Fit gym to hit my numbers. I also need to open five regional gyms and sell ten franchises to hit my $4 million number. I can do that over the next five years."

Those are game plans. They aren't guarantees, but they are realistic strategies.

What's your game plan? What's the best game plan you could imagine—one from your Sweet Spot? How might you actually make that happen?

You may or may not have the answer to that right now. Once again— get help! Lots of people will be happy to help you figure it out. In fact, there are lots of people living in their Sweet Spot with their game plans for building wealth, doing just that—helping *you* figure it out! (I've found that most people in their Sweet Spot are all about helping others get into their own Sweet Spot.)

You can also have a plan for what you would need to create financial freedom in your *current* line of work, while planning out a strategy for creating financial freedom from your Sweet Spot. That way, you've got plan A (Sweet Spot wealth) and plan B (whatever you are doing now).

At this point in the book, you know the life you want, you know why you want it, you know what's holding you back, you know your numbers, you know your Sweet Spot, and you know the various methods of building wealth. Get in the game. Pick one and give it your all! Pick a couple and go for it!

This is still America. Even though most people don't do it, nothing's stopping *you*. In fact, millions and millions of people have done it before you. Millions and millions after you will do it. Rather than ask, "why not me?" ask yourself a much more powerful question. "Why me?" Find your answer. And then, do it.

To summarize: get clear about what you are going to do to have an increasing net worth each year. Are you gradually going to save relatively small amounts over a relatively long time period? Great! Tons of millionaires did it that way. Or are you going to build something (a money machine) and find a buyer for it? Great! Tons of investors are looking for just that machine. Or are you going to build a machine that kicks out an income for you, and just hang on to it (setting it up to require little of your active effort?) Super! Sounds awesome. Are you going to broker several big deals? Go for it. Are you going to build something beautiful (art, music, a building) and sell that? Fun! Do you stand to inherit enough money to live on? Woohoo! Great!

Whatever it is, get clear about *HOW* you are going to get from wealth point A to wealth point B.

If you don't have that plan, you'll never create financial freedom (other than through luck).

Saving and Investing

Since a good portion of readers will choose to build wealth by building up savings, here are some thoughts to get you started. There are a million books out there about how to save and invest, so I won't take up pages here teaching you.

1. **Make it Automatic**. Your chances of accumulating the savings you want to be financially free will be massively higher if you make saving automatic. You've heard it before: **pay yourself first**.

    This is a great time to check in on an important distinction: You know *what* to do, but are you *doing* what you know? It's pretty simple: right now, as you read, do you have an automatic savings program taking money from your income and diverting it into an account for savings? If you don't, get really clear—you're probably going to fail at earning and saving. If you do have automatic savings set up, well done!

    In either case, it's important to run some savings numbers with a financial planner (or at the very least with a retirement savings calculator online) to get a sense of how much you need to be saving. If it's a lot more than you are saving now, make a plan to ramp that savings up, month-by-month, over a year or two to get on track.

    The fear of being deprived in your life right now will be an obstacle to that. Your brain is wired to fear current deprivation more than to fear a future without enough resources. Know that, account for it and make a game plan to get on track. There are tons of communities dedicated to living more on less. Get into them—they are fun and inspiring. Google "simplicity movement" to learn more.

    How much should you be saving? That's so dependent on your particular situation, it's hard to answer. But to give you a general idea, most people should aim to save 15–20% of their income.

2. **Keep Some Safe:** What should you do with the savings? First, especially if in retirement, keep safe any money you might need in the next 3–5 years. Don't subject yourself to the mental anguish

of worrying about whether that money will be there or not. Make sure that it will be. You may need to forego some growth on it. So be it. We could debate this all day long, but I'm speaking from years of watching the reality of how clients react to having "near-term money" at risk, and it's not pretty. Don't do it.

3. **Do you NEED growth?** Next, for any money that you won't need for at least years, ask yourself this: Do I *NEED* to expose this money to risk in order to live the life I want? I'm sometimes amazed by how much risk some clients believe they need to take. It's the "cultural norm" for the wealthy to have their money exposed to risk, thus most people do the same. Yet if you can accomplish all of your goals and more without putting your money at risk of significant investment loss, why would you do that? You might find great reasons to do that, but it should not be a default starting point.

Why expose your money to risk? Clearly, for the potential reward. For the return on investment. Be clear: "return on investment" is the same as saying, "the hope for more with the risk of less—sometimes *way* less." Have a really good reason for taking that risk.

Many wealthy clients will find that their standard of living is well assured even in the face of investment loss and decide that exposing part of their assets to risk offers them the potential to give more to charity, leave more to their family, or to fund specific visions. That's great and makes fine sense.

Other folks will find it hard to accumulate enough assets to fund their desired lifestyle without the "tailwind" of investment returns.

It's really important that you determine for yourself (or better, with help) to what extent you might need and want investing returns, and be willing to ride that experience, through ups and downs, pros and cons.

4. **Address Inflation**: In any case, one of the main reasons to invest is the quest to outpace the ravaging effects of inflation. While it's common to interpret inflation as the general rising of prices, inflation is actually the falling value of money as more and more currency (technically, credit) is infused into our economy by the Fed. To oversimplify, the more dollars there are, the less each is worth. (It's kind of like frequent flier miles.)

Putting your money to "work" by lending it or by owning assets with the potential and expectation of growth in value has historically been about the best way to maintain the purchasing power of your money.

5. **Invest**: Investing is a massively complex topic. Yet let me simplify it down to its essence:

- As an investor, you want the maximum return for the lowest risk.
- Any opportunity you have to increase return for the same risk, or decrease risk for the same return, should look attractive.
- Generally speaking, risk and return will go hand in hand. Exceptions are rare or non-existent.
- Choose your level of risk carefully. The market crash of 2008 probably taught you that.
- When you invest, you expose your money to a "driver of return." In other words, you place your money somewhere that offers you a good *reason* to expect there to be more money later.

And you assess that *likelihood* and determine whether that's acceptable to you.

For example, when you invest in bonds, you expect to be paid by others for the privilege of using your money. When you buy stock, you buy a piece of a company and expect that the company's increasing earnings, combined with the investing public's sustained desire to pay (a multiple) for those earnings, will grow your investment. When you invest in land, you expect that the supply and demand for that land will lead to higher prices. When you buy gold, you expect that supply and demand will lead to higher prices. When you invest in timber, you expect that the wood sold will bring more than the cost to plant, raise and harvest it.

- Every "investment" has its own drivers of returns. Diversify those as much as possible. Owning U.S. and foreign stocks offers you diversification of individual companies and countries, but stocks fundamentally share the same drivers of returns. That's not great diversification.

  Don't leave the juicy bits on the table. It's really easy to design a portfolio that takes an unnecessary amount of risk for the return it offers (or offers low return for the risk it takes). There are some really powerful ways to "squeeze the juice" from a portfolio right down to "the rind."

- The classic example is through the "magic of diversification." Briefly stated, you can create a situation where you get both higher return *and* lower risk by combining investment A with investment B than you would with either investment on its own. Did you get that?

- I'll make up numbers to illustrate: if Investment A historically offered 8% annual return, and investment B offered 10% return, it's possible to combine them to get a 12% annual return. PLUS—to have done it at lower risk than either A or B incurred on its own. Higher return for lower risk? What?

- It's counterintuitive, but mathematically sound. The Moral: diversify broadly across many asset classes and drivers of return to take advantage of this "magic." It may be the only free lunch in investing.

- **Don't try this at home**: To be blunt, chances are that you're bad at investing, even if you are smart. I say that because studies prove it. And I've witnessed my super-intelligent clients' misguided inclinations. Google "Dalbar Study" to read about the research this organization conducted to illustrate that, on average, investors underperform on the market by about 6% annually. That's to say that they shot themselves in the foot by losing about 6% of the annual return that was available to them. Why? Emotional investing; market timing; chasing returns. A bunch of reasons, but namely—people are terrible at investing. Our exploration of obstacles illustrated the behavioral biases we have that lead to poor decision-making, and it plays out painfully in the typical investor.
  - Not you? What makes you so sure? Investing is an extremely complex subject; we're constantly bombarded by the industry and the media with counterproductive (and unrealistic) messages that success lies in picking stocks and timing the market; our brains are wired to make poor calls and our emotions lead to poor decisions. If you are going to invest on your own, get really educated—study the daylights out of it. Or, if this isn't your passion, get help.

- Finally, **financial planning isn't all about the investments**. This whole book asserts that. People so often put all their energy into trying to mess with their portfolios, yet have not taken care of all the fundamentals (knowing what they want, having an asset building strategy, insurance planning, estate planning, etc.). Don't lose the forest for the trees. A portfolio is just a tool. I've *never* seen a portfolio make someone happy. Much more common is to attach our emotions to the ups and downs of the markets and to then act emotionally based on fear (sell!) and greed (buy!). **Your life fulfillment will have had relatively little to do with your portfolio. Take beautiful care of it, but make sure you broaden your focus to include all the other important stuff.**

Perhaps I'll write a different book on investing someday. I haven't provided enough "How-to" to do this on your own, as that's not my intent here. For now, I just wanted to make a handful of points that I hope will help you on your journey.

In summary: To get from point A (your current net worth and income) to point B (your desired net worth and income), you are going to have to do something specific to grow your net worth. There are only a handful of ways to do it. Get clear and pick one (or more). And to the greatest extent you can, pick one that allows you to "live Woohoo!" and build wealth from your Sweet Spot. More than anything, deliver massive value to the world, value that people crave, and you will supercharge your journey to financial freedom.

CHAPTER 10

Pillar #6: Get Help

Aaaaaaahhhhh! Look at all the things you're supposed to do! Get in the game, figure out what you want, differentiate your spirit from your ego, ignore the critic, explore your brain, crunch numbers, calculate needs, save money, build a business, invest wisely… aaahhh! Help!!

Yes. Get help.

Keep doing what you've always done, and you'll keep getting what you've always gotten. A big reason you aren't farther right and higher up on the Woohoo! Wealth graph is because you're trying to do too much of it yourself and foregoing the powerful help available to you.

The world is full of people who have surmounted obstacles you face and who are more than happy to share their experience and wisdom with you. Some may be friends or mentors who do it for free. Others may be highly-trained professionals who charge. Either way, use them! It's good for you; it's good for them; it's good for the world.

Clearly, we live in a culture where asking for help (especially for men) feels like a sign of weakness. Paradoxically, I'm sure that you've found that anytime a person has come to you for help, you've ended up feeling more connected with and respectful of that person.

As counterintuitive as it is, we don't connect with each other through our strengths and perfections as much as we do through our weaknesses, problems, openness, and vulnerability.

Asking for help is a rewarding human experience. Gratitude usually emerges as a result, and that's about as lovely a human experience as you can have.

What kind of help?
1. Coaching.
2. Counseling.
3. Community.

Coaching

Coaches are some of the greatest people you'll meet. Trained life or business coaches help you perform at your best. They help you clarify what you want, what's standing in the way, and what actions you can take to make progress.

They tend to rely on *your* wisdom for the right answers and on *their* understanding of people and life to guide you to it. If you've never had a coach, you are missing out. Good coaches hold you higher than you hold yourself, they see you for who you really are, and they cheerlead the hell out of you. And it feels fantastic. They can also crack the whip for you if you want that too.

In this process, whenever you hit an obstacle that you feel has to do with knowing what you want and having the courage to go for it, think coaching. If you want to get inspired and still be practical, think coaching. If you want someone to call you on your BS, ask a coach to.

The Coaches Training Institute is the leading coach training organization. They are at **www.thecoaches.com** and have a find-a-coach feature. The International Coach Federation (ICF) **www.coachfederation.org** is the coaching industry association and can also help you find a coach.

There are plenty of coach training organizations—some are totally flaky and others are really great. The main thing to do is to identify a few coaches and try a coaching session with them. Most offer that without cost. A majority work by phone. If you finish inspired with new possibility, you've likely found a great coach. If you thought it was weird, maybe that's not the coach for you.

You are also welcome to check in with me (**Colin@DrakeWealth.com**) to see if I have any spaces open in my coaching calendar. I'd *love* to help you on this journey!

Counseling

Here, I'm thinking of two kinds of counseling.

The first is professional advice on business and financial topics. You've got some financial planning to do. Get help! Look for a Certified Financial Planner® who offers true financial planning (not just lame printouts in an effort to sell you stuff). There are tons of great ones out there. Check the Financial Planning Association website (**www.fpanet.org**) to find a planner. Go to the Kinder Institute website **www.kinderinstitute.com** and click on "Find a Financial Life Planner" to find Registered Life Planners®, all of whom are trained in helping you through this kind of process.

Creating wealth is SO much more likely when you have experts helping you make great decisions.

My business, Drake Wealth Management (which can be found at **www.DrakeWealth.com**) is dedicated to helping you do everything

I've described in this book. Contact me; I'd love to help! In addition to financial planning, coaching and wealth management, I offer powerful products and programs designed to rocket you into Woohoo! Wealth. My flagship program is the Woohoo! Wealth Weekend—over three days, we get you charged, we create a game plan, and we launch. And it's a total blast (pun intended!)

The other kind of counseling I'm talking about is psychological. If you can see that you are stuck and suspect that it's not something you are going to unstick on your own, get someone to help you.

Wherever you can see that expertise will move you forward, shorten your journey, or help you avoid mistakes, seriously consider using it. You'll be glad you did. You might start with the belief that you can't afford to pay for professional advice. Here's another way to look at it: Can you afford *not* to pay for help?

Community

This is a really powerful and fun one. Get the support of your friends, family, and like-minded wealth builders. Tell them what you are up to, ask for their support, and tell them what kind of support would be helpful.

Most powerful is the community of people dedicated to the same thing you are. Sometimes, family members might feel threatened or envious that you are "going for it" and try to keep things status quo. On the other hand, people who want this just as much as you do are a fantastic community to be a part of. Find positive people in your life who want the best for you and will cheer you on and support you.

Come to our Facebook page, which can be found at **www.facebook.com/WoohooWealth**, and you'll be in community with other awesome people forging towards increasing aliveness and wealth. Come to a live

Woohoo! Wealth Weekend event, and you'll swim in the energy of great people like you who are pumped to make this happen.

Recent studies have shown that we tend to be the average of the five people we spend the most time with. Look at those five people, average their income, and that's likely to be your income. It's the same with weight, etc. Choose your company wisely. Associate with positive people, wealthy people, and alive people. Life's way more fun that way!

> *"Keep away from people who try to belittle your ambitions. Small people always do that, but the really great make you feel that you, too, can become great."*
>
> **Mark Twain**

To sum up: Going it alone is a bad call. The world is full of great helpers, and you will dramatically increase your chances of success by relying upon others to help get you there.

ACTION

Make a list of three immediate steps you could take to get help. It might include asking your spouse for support in this quest for Woohoo! Wealth. It might be making a call to try out a coach. It might be registering for a Woohoo! Wealth Weekend at www.WoohooWealth.com.

Get on it. Start to build your support team.

And remember, as you look to your world: We love you! We want your success! We want you to be wealthy! We love your aliveness! We want to help in any way we can! Just ask! We're ready and waiting to support you.

CHAPTER 11
Pillar # 7: Be Courageous

ACTION

Get a sheet of paper. Draw a medium-sized circle on the left side. Now draw a large circle on the right side. Now, inside the smaller circle on the left, write the words "My Comfort Zone". Inside the larger circle to the right, write "Where Woohoo! happens." Remember that.

A little Journey...

I want to invite you to come along on a little journey with me...

First, I would like you to imagine yourself standing in a cemetery. Yup—a graveyard. Even better, if you can, actually go stand in a real one. If you can't do that, pull up a picture of one and imagine yourself standing in it.

Look around.

They are all dead. Dead! Gone. Finished. Game over. Spent. Life no more.

Under each tombstone lies the remains of a human life. A person who walked the earth with hopes and dreams, fears and demons, and strengths and weaknesses. A person who had friends and family. A person who got emotionally wounded over and over. A person who experienced terrible embarrassment. A person who was in love, and who had high hopes for life. A person who experienced triumph and joy. A person who felt shame and defeat.

There lies the disintegrated shell of what once carried a soul through this world. And all that soul wanted was to really *live!*

Like a kid riding a slow donkey in a race and kicking it to go faster, each soul dug into its human and said, "Go. Go! C'mon! Go, God damn it! Live!"

And the person replied, "I am!"

And the soul said, "Are you kidding? You think that's all you've got?"

And the person said, "Yeah—that's all I've got."

And the soul cried out, "Are you f'in *kidding* me? You ain't seen *nothin'* yet! You're just getting *started!* C'mon—go for it…LIVE! Let's DO this!"

And the person replied, "But I'm *scared!*"

And the soul said, "Of *course*, you are! That's the whole point! If you couldn't feel fear, you couldn't feel joy, love, triumph, and aliveness! That's the *game* you are in: Life awaits you… you are scared… and you are supposed to go for it anyway. That's life. Now LIVE! For crying out loud, kick it up a notch. I'm dying in here!!"

And the person said, "But what if…"

And the soul interrupted, "Arrghhh! Those three words are killing me more than any in the human language. Please! What if? I'll tell you what if. The second worst-case scenario is—you die! The *worst*-case scenario is you never actually *live!* Now come on—let's get living!"

And the person replied, "Stop harassing me. I'm living just fine. I like my life as it is."

And the soul said, "What's the point of owning a Ferrari if you are going to drive in the slow lane? What's the point of having wings if you aren't going to fly? What's the point of being a sailing ship if you sit in harbor rather than sail to great adventures? I did not come to you to be 'fine, OK, good, medium, all right'. Do you know what it took to get here?! I came for the ride! I'm here to live it all, to take it all in, to thrive, to grow, to learn, to fail, to succeed. I'm here to know the depths of love. I'm here to glow, to radiate, to *everything*!"

And the person replied, "Well how the hell am I supposed to do that?"

And the soul replied, quite simply, "Just listen to me. And please do as I say."

There, in the ground, lie literally billions of people. Most of them didn't listen. The fear was too great, and they lived decent lives.

And there also lie the courageous ones who said, "OK. Fuck it. Let's do this! What's first?" And then they listened. And acted.

Your quest for Woohoo! Wealth is an extraordinary journey. It is literally out of the ordinary. In it lies your self-actualization. In it lies your road to triumph—to becoming all of who you are capable of being and all that your spirit is calling you to be. In it is your ticket to the life you most deeply yearn to live. Your quest for Woohoo! Wealth is your path to True Wealth!

You *should* be scared shitless. If you aren't, you haven't been listening closely enough to your inner calling. Being scared is the sign that you are on the right track. Being scared is aliveness. Relish it! Great things are afoot when you are scared.

I'm terrified of looking bad, making a fool of myself, of being reject-ed, of letting my family down, of making costly mistakes, and of being judged. And, I'm even more afraid of dying having never really lived!

> *"Men spend their lives in anticipations, in determining to be vastly happy at some period when they have time. But the present time has one advantage over every other—it is our own. Past opportunities are gone, future have not come. We may lay in a stock of pleasures, as we would lay in a stock of wine; but if we defer the tasting of them too long, we shall find that both are soured by age."*
>
> **Charles Caleb Colton**

The only thing that stands between you and the life and wealth you have always wanted is excuses. That's it.

"I'm scared" is an excuse.

"My parents didn't teach me about money" is an excuse.

"I can't do it right now because…" is an excuse.

"I have too much on my plate" is an excuse.

"I'm not smart enough" is an excuse.

"I'm pretty happy" is an excuse.

"I don't really want it" is an excuse (and a lie).

Of course, you have obligations. But you are also endowed with the potential to discover how to succeed, even *with* obligations.

Your spirit lies in wait for you to get your act together and kick your life up a notch. It's waiting for you to pull the cotton out of your ears and hear what it's telling you: "I want to LIVE. Live large! I want to *give*! I want passion and energy."

When you think about it, all we really have in life is our energy: Our physical energy, mental energy, emotional energy, and spiritual energy. Woohoo! Wealth is having bountiful energy in all areas of your life.

You're on a mission. You're an adventurer and an explorer. You are making tracks towards a land few people know. You are swimming hard upstream against the current of mainstream society.

I challenge you: Be courageous!

Courage doesn't mean you don't have fear. Courage is acting in the face of fear. Doing it *despite* being scared.

Look at those dead people lying there. Ask them: How do you live life in the face of fear, complacency, apathy, and mediocrity? How do you break out of your comfort zone and bust into thriving? Listen, and you'll hear their answers, because that's actually your soul answering for you. You know everything you need to know. Just ask and listen.

You are equipped with a perfectly functioning internal GPS that is telling you where to go next. Your heart knows what you want. Just ask it. It *really and truly* is that simple.

Visiting an Old Friend...

Now, for a moment, let's leave this graveyard and go visit somebody else...

For this one, I want you to imagine yourself standing on the doorstep of the house in which you grew up. Whether or not it still exists today, imagine standing at the front door as you are now.

Look around; remember the colors, the smells, and the view. Remember how the doorbell sounded? Remember who your neighbors were? Put your ear to the door and listen. Notice something astonishing… you hear your family inside (as in mother, father, sibling, or whomever you grew up with there). Look behind you for a moment—one of your childhood friends just rode by on a bike and waved. That friend is 8 years old. As you wrestle with the time warp you are in, the door opens.

Staring up at you is…you.

You at 8 years old.

The 8-year-old you instantly recognizes the adult you and, after the shock wears off, warmly embraces you. You sit down together to talk. There, you sit looking into the face of the you you once were. The one who had unlimited dreams for what life would hold in store. The one who knew you could be anything you wanted when you grew up. The you who laughed hysterically with ease. The you whose heart was open and generous. The you who was passionate about life.

Look at yourself squarely in the eye, and tell this little person how it turns out when they get to be your age. What lays in store for that little you? How are you doing delivering on the dreams entrusted to you? Tell young you who you have become. Account for yourself.

Watch the expression of the little you as you describe who you have become and how you are spending your days. What does the little you seem to think about the news you come bearing? What's it like, at that age, for the little you to look into the future and compare your life to what they hoped it held in store?

Please actually close your eyes now and visualize this.

You might find your little you jumping for joy and thrilled to hear it. You might see a heartbroken, crestfallen little child. You might see a temper tantrum and anger. Notice what you see.

And now... GET IT! Hear the message from your little you (once again, your spirit). Listen. What's it trying to tell you? How are you doing? What do you really want?

More importantly, what's next? Look your little you in the eyes and make yourself a promise. Tell your little you what's ahead from today onward. If the life you already described thrilled the little you, then talk about the next heights to which you are taking yourself. If you made your little you cry, tell them how you are going to do better.

And then, go do it!

Your spirit is, with infinite love and patience, awaiting your courage to live the life you really want to live.

The life that will have your soul looking down at your grave and saying, "Well done, my friend. Well done. Thank you."

Your child you is sending you signals through time to please have the courage to get clear about what you want and to make it real—they really want to have a fabulous life.

> *"Twenty years from now you will be more disappointed by the things that you didn't do than by the ones you did do. So throw off the bowlines. Catch the trade winds in your sails. Explore. Dream. Discover."*
>
> **Mark Twain**

When you think about it, pretty much the entire universe is inviting you to go for it. There may be a few "bah humbugs" out there, but they are massively outnumbered by your cheering section. What are you waiting for? Stop getting ready to live and start really doing it!

> *"Life is either a daring adventure or nothing."*
>
> **Helen Keller**

I want to challenge you to make a courageous decision, *right now*. Before you even turn this page, decide one thing you are going to do *today* to take a step on the path to Woohoo! Wealth! Write it down, call a friend and tell that person that you just committed to taking that action, and ask for accountability. Then do it. It all starts with one small step, then another, then another.

Please join me is this quest to live life by inspired design, to find your Woohoo! and to reach to ever grander heights of aliveness and YOUness, to build all the financial wealth you want, to supercharge your adventure, to build Woohoo! Wealth. We won't ever regret it. We'll forever be grateful.

With immense love, best wishes, and congratulations, I sign off.
Live on!
Wooooooooohhhhhhhhhhhhhhooooooooo!!!!!!!!!!!!!!

Colin

EPILOGUE

The Parable of You at the Pearly Gates

Your soul approaches the proverbial "Pearly Gates." There, to your surprise, has gathered a council of some pretty heavy hitters: Jesus, Mohammed, Buddha, Gandhi, and Mother Theresa. As you look around, you begin to see that you recognize every face. It's everybody you ever met, knew or learned about. They welcome you and ask you to stand before them.

"Hey, welcome back! Great to see you. What a pleasure it's been to watch you. Great go around! Well done. All right, before you settle back in here, we have to do our usual feedback survey. How'd we do?"

"What do you mean, how'd you do?" you ask.

"You know, in game design? Did we make it too easy, too hard? Should we have turned up the fear factor a little more, or would less have allowed you to really have a better ride? Did we throw in too many emotional wounds? Did we throw you off enough with media?"

"I'm not following…"

"Dear beloved one, your only mission was to become as authentically you and as radiantly alive as possible. To bring to the world the full magnificence of who you are. Everything else was just details. Did we make that too hard or too easy? Or just right?"

"Ohhhh. Yeah. Yes. Yes. Yes. I remember that now. Well, let me think…" You reply.

"It was really hard. No doubt about it. But you know, it was totally doable. Once I gave myself permission and mustered up the courage, I sure had a hell of a good ride (I can say 'hell' here, can't I?). I'd say it's magnificent. Maybe it takes folks a few go-arounds to start to get the rules of the game, but they can definitely figure them out. You certainly left enough clues! Nah—I'd say it's genius; in fact, it's perfect. I'm ready for another go!"

"Good. Good. Glad to hear it. Well played, my friend. Sure—have another go—you'll be a great light among them. Lead the way. Shine. Love. Live."

Hey you. Yes, you! This is your go. Lead the way. Shine. Love. Live.

ABOUT THE AUTHOR

Colin Drake loves life. His passion and mission is to inspire and instruct others in the quest for wealth and aliveness.

Founder of Drake Wealth Management, a boutique wealth management and financial life planning firm, he guides clients to financial peace, security and thriving. His Woohoo! Wealth training programs are dedicated to offering everyone access to the perspectives, strategies and tactics of living large and building wealth doing it.

Colin is a Certified Financial Planner®, Registered Life Planner® and Wealth Coach. He's spent the last fifteen years on the front lines of guiding the nation's wealthiest individuals to personal and financial success.

Colin is a husband to a fantastic and gorgeous wife, Rebecca. He's the glowingly proud father of the glorious Delphine and the fabulous Morgan.

Colin is a prankster, a surfer, a photographer, a drummer, a world traveler, a chef, a paraglider, a Frenchman, a workshop junkie, and, in high school, was voted "Most likely to be a windsurfing instructor at Club Med." He did end up teaching windsurfing and living in Maui for a while, but not at Club Med. So there!

He can be found at **www.DrakeWealth.com** and at **www.WoohooWealth.com**.

You can contact him at **Colin@DrakeWealth.com**.